GREAT

Figures

◆IN◆ HISTORY

David L. Martin
Artwork by Michelle Beidler and Peter Balholm

Lamp and Light Publishers, Inc.
Farmington, New Mexico, U.S.A.

ISBN-13: 978-1-61778-122-3
ISBN-10: 1-61778-122-3

Lamp and Light Publishers, Inc.
26 Road 5577
Farmington, New Mexico 87401

© 2020 Lamp and Light Publishers, Inc.
All rights reserved
First printing 2020
Printed in the United States of America

Table of Contents

Introduction 7
The Greatest Figure of All 9

Buddha
   Founder of Buddhism 13

Confucius
   Leader of Chinese Thought 19

Polycarp
   Early Church Leader 23

Constantine
   Freedom for Christians 29

Augustine
   New Errors for Old Heresies 37

Patrick
   "Apostle" to Ireland 43

Muhammed
   The Birth of Islam 47

Peter Waldo
   The Waldensians 53

John Wycliffe
   Morning Star of the Reformation 59

Table of Contents

Martin Luther
The Reformation Begins in Germany...............65

The Radical Trio
The Swiss Brethren Forge Ahead 72

Michael Sattler
A Sign in the Fire...............................79

Menno Simons
A Good Name for the Anabaptists...............83

John Calvin
A TULIP Takes Flower.........................89

John Knox
The Reformation Comes to Scotland.............97

Henry VIII
The Reformation Begins in England 101

William Tyndale
A New Bible for English Readers 107

Jacob Arminius
A Calvinist Who Changed His Mind 113

John Bunyan
A Pilgrim Who Progressed 117

William Penn
The Man Pennsylvania Was Not Named After 123

Isaac Newton
A Dreamer Who Made Good....................129

John Wesley
The Methodist Movement Is Born 137

Table of Contents

Isaac Watts
Father of English Hymnody 143

William Carey
Father of Modern Missions...................... 147

Charles Finney
Lawyer Turned Evangelist 153

Charles Darwin
A Book That Argued for Evolution.............. 159

David Livingstone
"I Will Open a Path Through the Country" 165

Karl Marx
Father of Communism 173

George Mueller
Quiet Faith in a Dependable God 179

Dwight Moody
A Simple Gospel for Multitudes 187

Fanny Crosby
A Poet Who Gave Herself Away................... 195

Charles Taze Russell
Founder of Jehovah's Witnesses 201

Martin Luther King, Jr.
Civil Rights Leader 207

Billy Graham
International Evangelist 215

The Forgotten Figures of History 221

INTRODUCTION

Let us clear up a few possible misunderstandings.

First, just because these people were great (in the sense that they became well known) does not mean that they were all good models for us to follow. We should learn from people's good and bad points and imitate what is worthwhile.

Secondly, you need not aspire to be great like any of these persons. You should be as godly as you can be, but you need not stand head and shoulders above other godly people. Godliness is something we should work at together. Rather than praying to be a spiritual giant, pray "that we might all come . . . unto a perfect man, unto the measure of the stature of the fulness of Christ" (Ephesians 4:13).

By the way, some pictures you find here of people from early history are artist's concepts. We appreciate the efforts of Michelle Beidler and Peter Balholm.

We hope that as you read this book, you will enjoy becoming better acquainted with characters you may have already heard of, and perhaps meet persons you never heard of before. May the Lord bless your ventures.

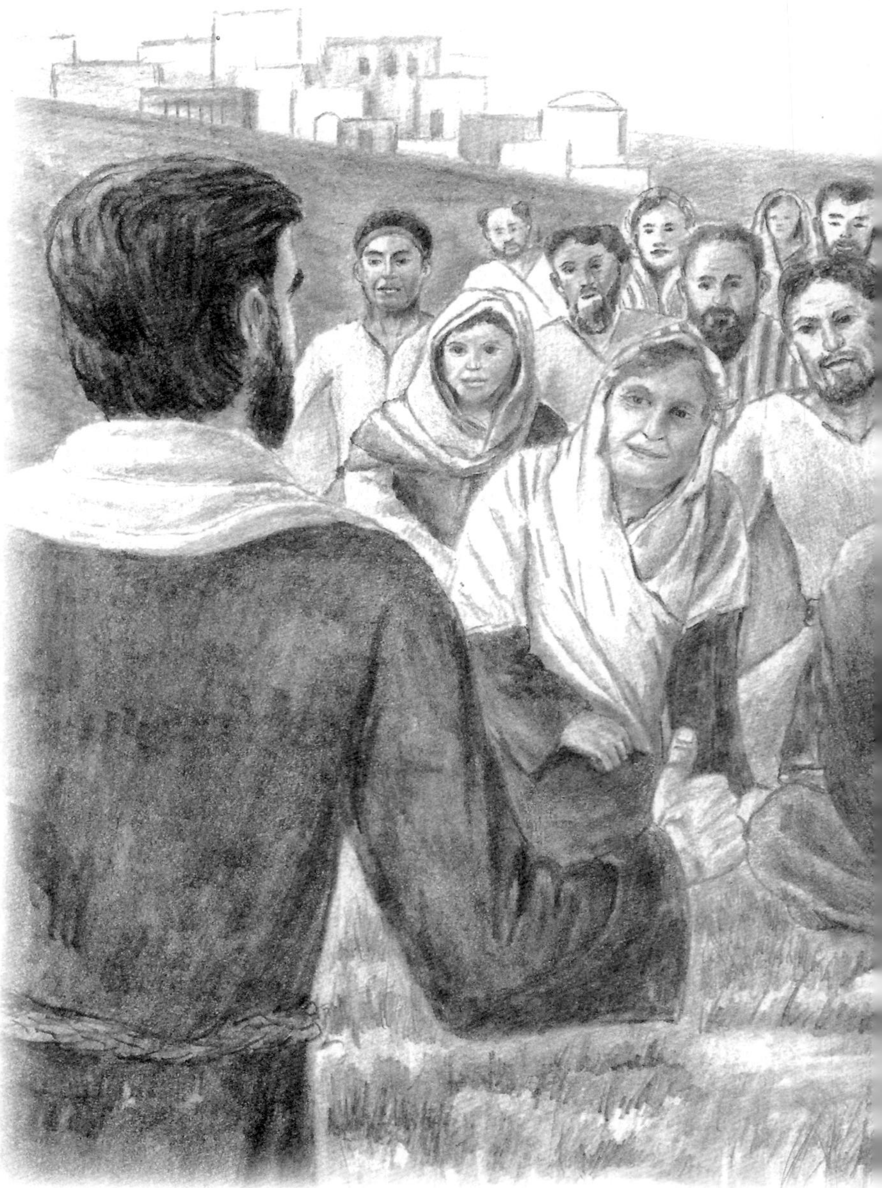

The Greatest Figure of All

He was the oldest of five brothers. He worked at His father's trade, and townspeople who dropped in at the shop treated Him much like any other neighbor boy. He learned the usual things at synagogue school. At age twelve He surprised the experts by how well He understood the Scriptures. After that though, He disappeared into ordinary family life again. Hardly anyone paid serious attention to Him until He was about thirty years old.

Suddenly His neighbors began hearing reports that He was preaching to crowds and healing sick people. They took it all with a grain of salt. After all, nothing special ever happened in their town, and no one famous ever came out of it!

When He did finally come back to visit His hometown and attend the synagogue, He preached well enough. But people's eyebrows went up when He claimed to be the very one Isaiah had prophesied about centuries before—in other

The Greatest Figure of All

words, the long-looked-for Messiah. He told them He knew they wouldn't believe it, and they didn't. They hustled Him out of the synagogue and would have killed Him, but somehow He slipped away.

He was good at slipping away. The quiet life suited Him best. Although He tolerated crowds, somehow He never saw them as crowds. He saw the individuals in them, and He made time on housetops, in gardens, and in private homes for as many as He could. He was a common man.

But He was great too. The longer people watched and listened, the more they realized that He was either the greatest pretender, or the greatest man, who had ever lived. Indeed, He claimed to be more than a man. "Before Abraham was, I am," He said. What were the people to do with a statement like that? Did they believe it or did they not? The people fell into two groups—those who believed in Him, and those who despised Him more and more.

At last the ones who hated Him got the upper hand. They took Him to court and had Him condemned and killed. But just a few days later, they heard that He was alive again. He had slipped out of their hands! Hundreds, and shortly thousands, of people believed that He had risen from the dead. Soon the movement, like a fire, was totally out of His enemies' control.

It still is. On every continent, we find men and women who follow the Lord Jesus Christ. They would die for Him, for if they died, would they not rise again? More than that, they live for Him, for has He not promised, "Lo, I am with you alway, even unto the end of the world"?

The Greatest Figure of All

Still more than that, they let Him live within them. Once they receive this greatest of all honors—Christ within their own hearts—they no longer care much where He assigns them. Preaching to thousands or cooking two eggs—what does it matter? Either one is a great assignment if they can do it hand in hand and heart to heart with the Lord. Either is a great privilege if it is accepted by Him, the greatest figure in history.

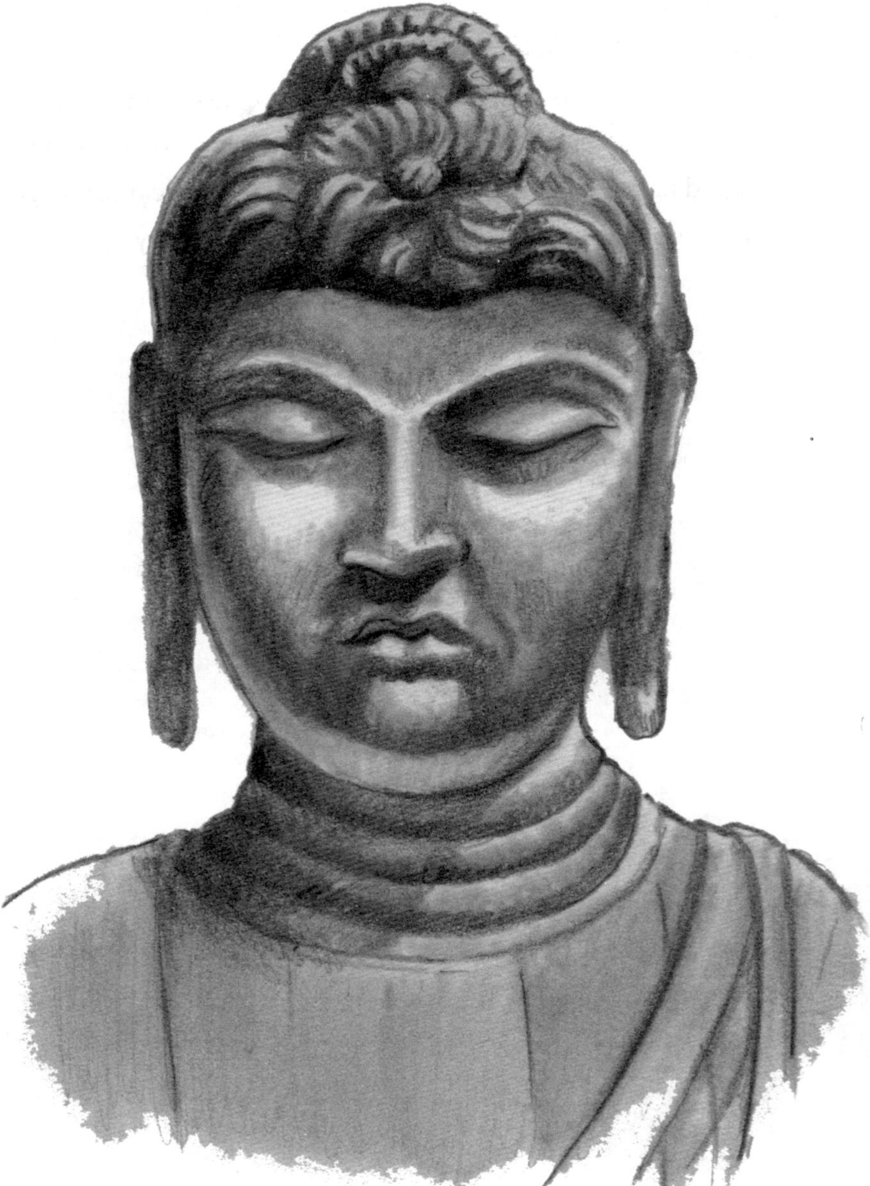

Buddha

Founder of Buddhism

(563?–483? BC)

His real name was Siddhartha Guatama. His followers called him Buddha, "Enlightened One," after he announced that the real meaning of life had dawned on him and he began preaching about it.

In order to understand Buddha, we must understand the world in which he grew up. It was a Hindu world, with thousands of gods but only one main spirit, called Brahman. Siddhartha grew up learning about reincarnation, the Hindu belief that when someone died, he was reborn as another person, or perhaps an animal. If a person had lived a good life, he would be reborn into a higher class, known as a caste. On and on the cycle of death and rebirth would go unless a person reached spiritual perfection. Then his soul would enter into rest.

Buddha...

We have more legends than facts about Siddhartha, but the usual story runs like this. He was born in what is now Tibet, near the border of India. He was a high-caste Hindu, and his parents could afford to keep him in palace luxury, sheltering him from the sufferings so common in the world around him. He married a princess, and they had a son.

But when Siddhartha was twenty-nine, he ordered his charioteer to take him through the streets of the city. There he saw four sights that impressed him. (Some versions say he had a series of four visions.) He saw a sick man covered with sores, a man tottering with age, a corpse being carried to its grave, and a holy man (Hindu monk). The first three sights shocked him. He had never stared suffering in the face like this before. The sight of the monk, who looked calm and serene, impressed him with the idea that he too should become a holy man. Perhaps in this way he could better understand the meaning of life and learn how to cope with suffering.

One night, he slipped into the room of his young wife and newborn son as they lay sleeping, gave them one last look, then tore himself away. From then on, he took the life of a poor, homeless, wandering holy man.

To better understand the meaning of life, he deliberately put himself through the worst of suffering. He ate less and less until he was down to a kernel of grain a day and people said they could see the outline of his backbone through his stomach. He pulled out his beard one hair at a time. For six or seven years he suffered, and then he had had enough. He was *not* finding the meaning of life just by making himself miserable.

... Founder of Buddhism

One day he sat down in the shade of a tree and vowed that he was not leaving the spot until he had found enlightenment. After forty days of deep meditation[1] while he fought the temptation to give up his search, some simple truths came to him, and at last he felt satisfied.

These are the Four Noble Truths:

1. Suffering is everywhere. It is part of life.
2. Suffering is caused by desiring what you should not have instead of desiring virtues like kindness and truthfulness.
3. Suffering can be relieved by turning away from wrong desires.
4. To turn away from wrong desires, follow the Noble Eightfold Path. Choose the right (1) understanding, (2) intention, (3) speech, (4) action, (5) livelihood, (6) thoughts, (7) self-control, and (8) contemplation.

Buddha preached that the best way to choose is the "Middle Road." In other words, do not go to the extreme of too much suffering nor the opposite extreme of too much pleasure. The good way is somewhere between.

Buddha spoke against the Hindu caste system. This teaching won many people to the Buddhist faith. He also preached that Buddhists should live in peace without harming other people or even animals. They sometimes use nonviolent protests if they need to get a point across.

---

[1] Some writers say four weeks; some say seven.

However, like Hindus, Buddha believed in reincarnation, in which after a person dies, he is reborn into some other person or creature. He taught that through meditation and living a good life, a person can finally reach *nirvana,* the perfect state, and then he will no longer have to be reborn. But when his followers asked exactly what nirvana is, Buddha refused to say. Perhaps he did not know himself.

For forty years, Buddha traveled around teaching. He seems to have been a calm, good-natured man. Once, the story goes, a foolish fellow scoffed at him until Buddha said, "Son, if someone is offered a gift but does not accept it, who does the gift belong to?" The youth replied, "The person who offered it." Buddha said, "I do not accept your abuse and request that you keep it for yourself."

The rainy season slowed his followers down, but wealthy people built teaching centers and monasteries where monks and nuns could come and study. To this day during rainy season, many boys shave their heads, dress in yellow robes, and become trainee monks. Each day they walk around in the community with bowls for the neighbors to fill with food. No neighbor resents this; they count it a privilege to serve in this way. A few boys later become monks for the rest of their lives, but most of them go back to normal living after a brief period.

The followers of Buddhism fall into several groups. Theravada Buddhists are the conservatives. They stick close to what Buddha taught. Mahayana Buddhists are the liberal, common-man type popular in many countries. We find one form of it in Tibet, where

... Founder of Buddhism

the monks wear red robes instead of yellow ones and the ceremonies are enthusiastic and noisy. (Perhaps you have seen pictures of the Potala Palace, a center of Tibetan Buddhism that is now a museum.) Zen Buddhism, which emphasizes meditation, is popular in Japan. Quite a few Buddhists in the United States practice Zen.

Buddhism and Christianity contradict each other on very important points.

- Buddhists have no particular god unless it is Buddha himself. Christians worship God through His Son Jesus Christ.
- Buddhists can follow Buddhism and at the same time follow some other religion like Confucianism or Taoism. Christians who try to follow some other religion find that they have strayed from Jesus Christ, who said, "I am the way."
- Buddhists believe that a person who does wrong is "unskillful." Christians believe that a person who does wrong is a sinner.
- Buddhists try to save themselves through meditation and good behavior. Christians let God save them through the blood of Jesus Christ. Then the Christian allows the Holy Spirit to direct his life along the path of holiness. *Follow peace with all men, and holiness, without which no man shall see the Lord* (Hebrews 12:14).

If you travel in Southeast Asia, China, or Japan, here and there you may find statues of Buddha sitting cross-legged, his eyes closed in meditation. It would be interesting to know what he might have said if he had met Jesus Christ.

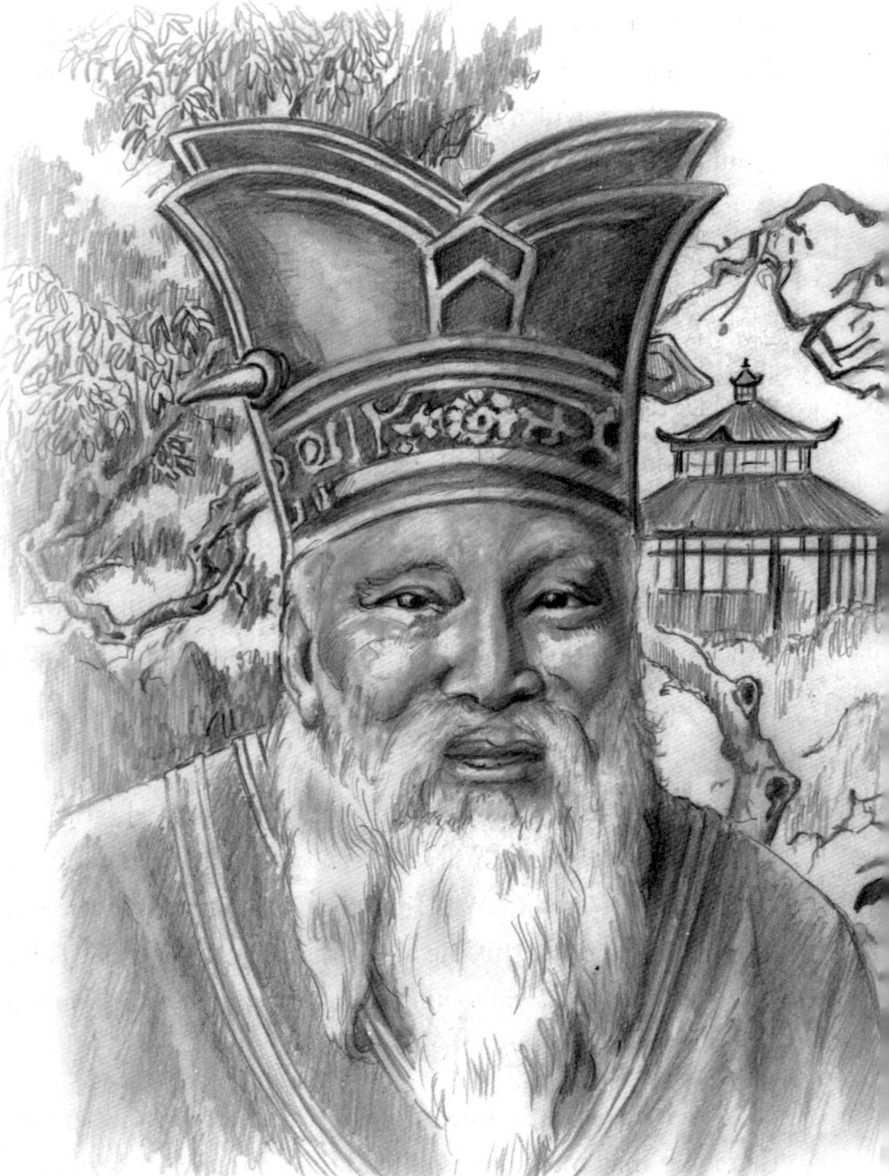

CONFUCIUS

LEADER OF CHINESE THOUGHT

(c. 551–479 BC)

Confucius, the Chinese philosopher, must have been an interesting man. But he lived so long ago, and so many legends swirl around him like fog, that it is hard to peer through and see who was really there. It was said that he had the back of a dragon, the lips of an ox, and a mouth like the sea. Where he governed, everyone became honest! Who indeed was the real Confucius?

When Confucius was born, his father was old. He died when Confucius was three. Life must have been difficult, for Confucius worked after school to support his mother. At age nineteen, he married, but a few years later he divorced his wife. There is no record that he married again.

He taught the way many teachers teach today, by insisting that his students figure some things out for themselves. He said,

CONFUCIUS...

"When I have presented one corner of a subject to any one, and he cannot from it learn the other three, I do not repeat my lesson." He had no time for lazy students, and even used a stick on them if necessary. He said, "Hard is the case of him who will stuff himself with food the whole day, without applying his mind to anything." But many students loved him, and he loved them. By the time his life closed, he had taught three thousand young men.

Confucius was modest in manner. He did not scoff at other teachers. He was not stubborn or opinionated. Although he kept his dignity as a teacher, Confucius must have had a sense of humor. Once when traveling, he and his students lost track of each other. But the students soon found him after a passerby told them he had seen a strange-looking man with the sad look of a stray dog. When Confucius heard the story, he was much amused.

He emphasized the wisdom of the ancestors, insisting that he did not say anything new, just passed on what already had been said. Much of what he had to say made good sense. He taught citizens to respect their government leaders, wives to respect their husbands, and the young to respect their elders. In turn, he said, leaders must be kind and good to those who follow them. He taught that good societies depend on good families, and good families upon good individuals. If individual persons are good, their families will be good, their government will be good, and the world will be good.

However, about God he had little to say. He refused to answer questions about the life to come. Although some of his statements sound like the words of Jesus, what he taught was more of a philosophy than a religion. One of his most famous statements is "Do not do to others what you would not have them do to you."

The teachings of Confucius spread far after he died. In fact, he was one of the most influential men who ever lived. His teachings helped to keep the Chinese people stable and sensible. But while the people of other nations were eager to learn new things, the Chinese kept relearning old things. They stayed much the same for two thousand years.

Confucius was interested in governments. When he was given the opportunity to rule, he was so successful (the story goes) that crime disappeared and people from neighboring areas came flocking to live under his government. But jealous officials put so much pressure on him that he sadly resigned. For thirteen years, he wandered from place to place, hoping to serve as advisor to government officials. At last, he was invited back to his home state, where he spent the last five years of his life quietly reading and writing. Toward the end, he was overheard singing,

> The great mountain must crumble,
> The strong beam must break,
> And the wise man wither away like a plant.

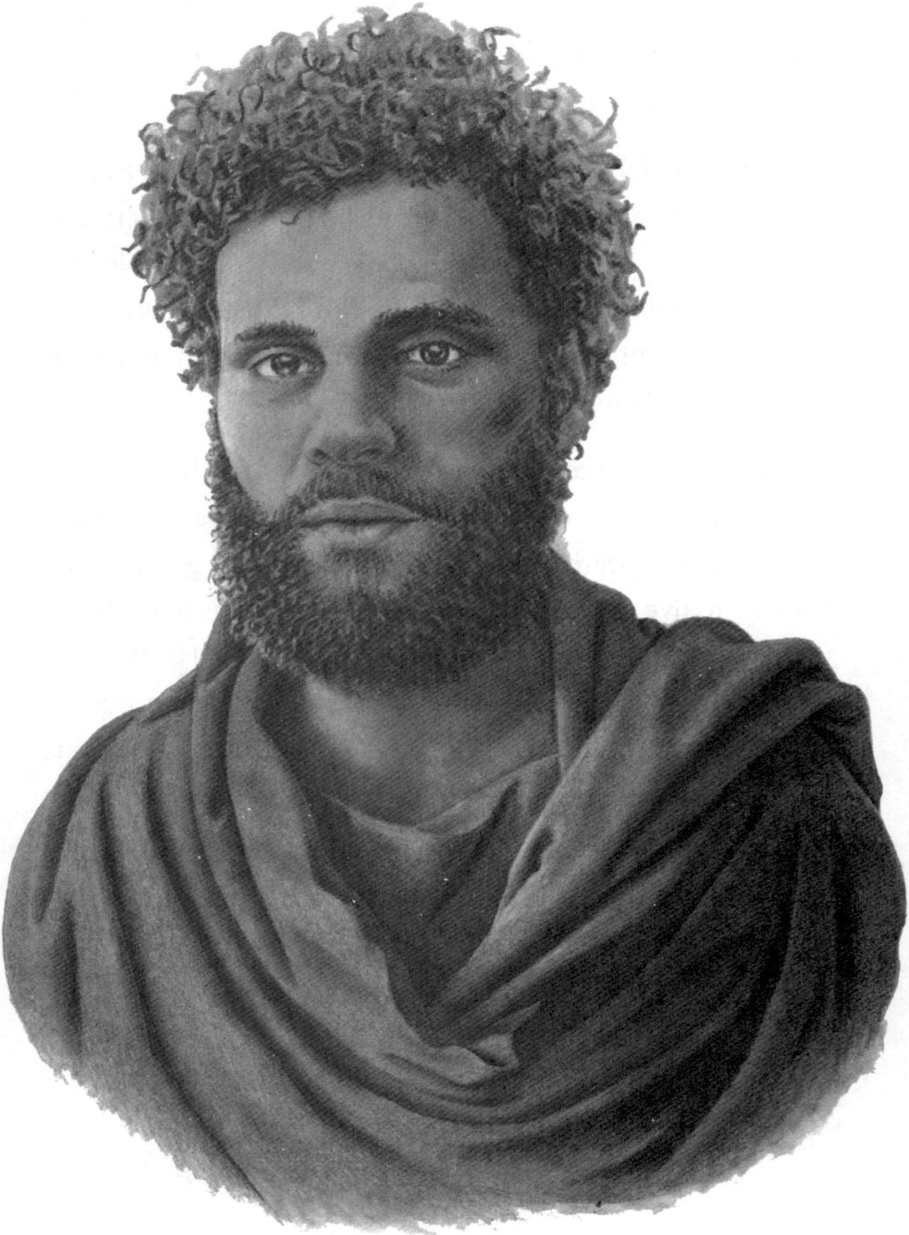

Polycarp

Early Church Leader

(AD 69?–155?)

Jesus' eleven apostles, and many others besides, spread the Gospel far and wide and paid for it with their lives. Tradition says that Matthew was beheaded in Ethiopia, Thomas was martyred in India, Peter was crucified in Rome, Barnabas was burned in Cyprus, and so on.

These early followers of Christ not only spread the Gospel, they also directed the new churches that had grown up wherever people had begun to follow Christ. In 2 Corinthians 11, the apostle Paul wrote about "the care of all the churches." One way Paul cared for the churches was to write to them. We have copies of his letters to the Corinthians, Galatians, and others. He wrote to the Romans before he ever got to see them.

As the apostles died, who shouldered the responsibility of leading the church? The Christians looked with special respect

Polycarp...

to those men who had been taught by the apostles. The last of these leaders, who lived to be a very old man, was Polycarp. He served as bishop in Smyrna, one of the seven churches to whom Jesus spoke in Revelation 2–3.

Polycarp must have drawn some very clear lines. One time when he met an old acquaintance named Marcion, who was teaching false doctrine, he began to pass by without speaking to him. Marcion said, "Don't you recognize me?" Polycarp replied, "I do indeed; I recognize the firstborn of Satan!" No doubt some heretics were offended by his plain talk, but it also won many of them over to embrace sound doctrine. Polycarp helped direct the church in Smyrna for many years.

Smyrna had an amphitheater where bloodthirsty audiences watched in fascination as gladiators battled each other to death or lions were turned loose on heretics to devour them. After they had watched a brave Christian named Germanicus lose his life, the watchers wanted more of the same. The cry went up, "Away with the godless! Fetch Polycarp!"

When Polycarp's friends heard this, they urged him to escape, so Polycarp moved out of Smyrna, but not very far. One night he dreamed that his pillow burst into flames. He told his friends that this must mean he would suffer as a martyr by fire.

When his pursuers finally caught up with him, Polycarp welcomed them in and offered them a meal, asking for an hour to pray before they took him away. The officers were bewildered by this kindly old man; they had come to arrest a dangerous public enemy! After granting him time to pray, they brought him to the city.

An official named Nicetes took him into his carriage, sat with him, and tried to persuade him to give up his faith. When Polycarp refused, Nicetes and his fellow officials began to threaten him. Then they put him out of the carriage so abruptly that he scraped his shin. An ancient church historian, Eusebius, quoted from a letter telling what took place next.

> But, as if nothing had happened, he set off happily and at a swinging pace for the stadium. There the noise was so deafening that many could not hear at all, but as Polycarp came into the arena a voice from heaven came to him: "Be strong, Polycarp, and play the man." No one saw the speaker, but many of our people heard the voice.
>
> His introduction was followed by a tremendous roar as the news went round: "Polycarp has been arrested!" At length, when he stepped forward, he was asked by the proconsul if he really was Polycarp. When he said yes, the proconsul urged him to deny the charge. "Swear by Caesar's fortune; say, 'Away with the godless!'" But Polycarp looked at all the crowd in the stadium and waved his hand towards them, sighed, looked up to heaven, and cried, "Away with the godless!" The governor pressed him further: "Swear, and I will set you free: execrate [curse] Christ." "For eighty-six years," replied Polycarp, "I

Polycarp...

have been His servant, and He has never done me wrong: how can I blaspheme my King who saved me?" "I have wild beasts," said the proconsul. "I will throw you to them, if you don't change your attitude." "Call them," replied the old man. "If you make light of the beasts," retorted the governor, "I'll have you destroyed by fire." Polycarp answered, "The fire you threaten burns for a time and is soon extinguished; there is a fire you know nothing about—the fire of the judgment to come and of eternal punishment. But why do you hesitate? Do what you want."

The proconsul was amazed, and set the crier to stand in the middle of the arena and announce three times, "Polycarp has confessed that he is a Christian." At this announcement the whole mass of [spectators], Gentiles and Jews alike, boiled with anger. A shout went up that Polycarp must be burned alive.

The crowds rushed to collect logs and faggots. The instruments prepared for the pyre were put around him, but when they were going to nail him to the stake, he cried, "Leave me as I am: He who enables me to endure the fire will enable me to remain on the pyre without shrinking."[2]

The letter added that after Polycarp had prayed aloud, men lit the fire, only to see it blazing up around his body without burning him. An executioner finally put him to death with the sword.

---

2   Eusebius, *The History of the Church*, tr. G. A. Williamson (New York, NY: Dorset Press, 1965), pp. 171–172. Condensed.

... Early Church Leader

Martyrs Mirror adds that twelve other Christians, who had come to Smyrna from Philadelphia, gave their lives for the Lord the same day. Although we do not know their names, we have the confidence that these faithful anonymous martyrs were received into glory just as warmly as Polycarp. This, of course, was the kind of thing Polycarp had worked all his life to accomplish.

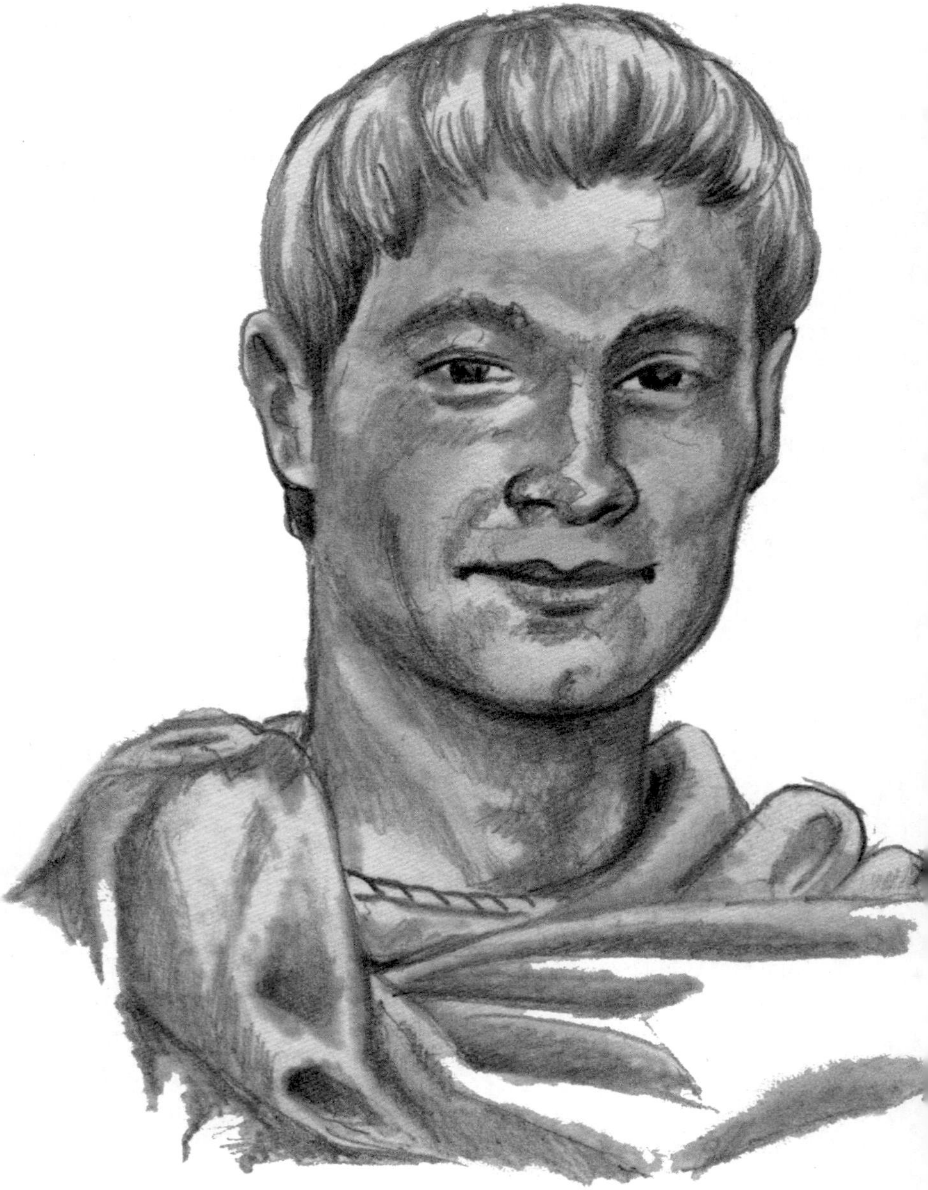

CONSTANTINE

FREEDOM FOR CHRISTIANS

(AD 272–337)

"Ye shall have persecution ten days," Jesus said in Revelation 2:10. Perhaps that was His way of saying that the early Christians under the Roman Empire would experience ten waves of persecution.

Why should the Roman government persecute the Christians? It didn't, at first. The Christians were just a small group, and no threat to the Roman Empire. At first, most persecution of the Christians came from Jews of that time. But as Christianity appealed to more and more people and spread from community to community, Roman leaders began to be concerned. What would happen to the old Roman ways if too many people became Christians? Would there be too much disloyalty to the government? Religious leaders were especially worried, because every time someone became a Christian, the old religions had one fewer worshiper. Also, citizens who did not know the Christians

Constantine...

well looked upon them with suspicion. When an illness struck a community or a storm hit, who knew but that the Christians had something to do with it?

During the first wave of persecution under the partly-insane Nero, the apostle Paul was beheaded and Peter was crucified. Many other Christians died by burning, being harried by dogs, and whatever other ways ingenious sinners could think of. The tenth wave of persecution, under the emperor Diocletian, was the worst. Churches were burned; Christians were banished or enslaved. Various Christians stood faithfully for their Lord in spite of being beaten savagely from head to toe, roasted in slow fires, tossed by wild beasts, and on and on. But there are other stories too, always briefly told, of Christians who suffered for a time and finally did give up their faith.

Then came Constantine.

Constantine began his career as a soldier like his father and worked his way up. The soldiers he commanded learned to like their young, handsome, and energetic officer. By the time the emperor died, Constantine was ready to make his bid for emperor. However, another contender for the throne, named Maxentius, stood in his way.

Constantine acted first. He and his army crossed the Alps and moved toward Rome. His army trapped Maxentius's army along the Tiber River, with no way to escape but across the Milvian Bridge.[3] The question was, could Maxentius's much

---

3 Will Durant, *The Age of Reason Begins* (New York, NY: Simon & Schuster, 1961), p. 654.

larger army, full of expert and experienced soldiers, fight their way out anyway and win against Constantine?

In later years, Constantine told his biographer, Eusebius, that he had seen in the sky a cross with the words, "In this sign conquer." The next day, his army slaughtered Maxentius's army. Maxentius and thousands of his soldiers ended up dead in the Tiber.

Supposedly impressed by the sign of the cross, in AD 313 Constantine issued the Edict of Milan, guaranteeing to "Christians and all others liberty to follow whatever form of worship they chose." At this point, Constantine ruled over the western part of the Roman Empire. To the east was a territory ruled by Licinius, who still persecuted Christians. But after Constantine defeated Licinius in AD 324, he became emperor of the whole Roman Empire. Eusebius wrote of this time, "Suddenly in less time than it takes to say it, those who a day or two before had been breathing death and threats were no more, and even their name was forgotten. . . . Light was everywhere, and men who once dared not look up greeted each other with smiling faces and shining eyes."[4]

Were the church's problems over? Not at all. Suddenly Christians were asking, "What shall we do with persons who compromised or gave up Christianity when we were being persecuted, and who now want to come back to the church? Should they come under discipline in some form?"

---

4 Eusebius, p. 413.

Constantine . . .

Some people said that after a time of proving, the offenders should be accepted freely back into the church. But others were not so sure, and they were especially concerned about what to do with church leaders who had failed. One bishop, named Donatus, insisted that such leaders be dismissed from office. He went so far as to say that the members those leaders baptized or ordained had not been baptized or ordained properly. When others did not agree with his hard line, Donatus started to set up leaders of his own choosing.

Constantine was troubled by issues like this. He had hoped that having Christians all over his empire would help to unify it and strengthen his government. But now Christians were splitting into rival groups.

An even bigger issue arose when a priest named Arius argued that if Jesus was the begotten Son of God, the Son could not have been co-eternal with the Father. This means He must have been created. Many people, such as the Jehovah's Witnesses, argue this way even today.

Arius overlooked the fact that Jesus existed long before He was begotten through Mary and became the human Son of God. Jesus Himself said, "Before Abraham was, I am." The old Christmas carol "O Come, All Ye Faithful" says it right: Jesus is "Son of the Father / Begotten, not created."

Constantine, as a political ruler, did not want such disunity in his kingdom. He wrote to the leaders of the opposing views, rebuking both sides for making a public ruckus over such a small question. Actually, it was a big question, but the uproar that arose over it was not Christian. Hoping to resolve the question, Constantine called for a great meeting of church leaders at Nicaea in what is now Turkey. Over three hundred bishops came, along with many other clergymen. After much debating, the council came down soundly in favor of the fact that Jesus is "of one substance with the Father." Constantine had gotten what he wanted. The church was more united now, except for a handful of dissenters. "Constantine celebrated the conclusion of the Council with a royal dinner to all the assembled bishops, and then dismissed them with the request that they should not tear one another to pieces."[5]

If you wonder what an emperor was doing trying to manage the church, other people wonder that too. The terms *church* and *Christian* have always meant different things to different people. In this book, we often use these terms in the broad sense, applying them to whoever called themselves Christian. The fact remains that Jesus said, "Not every one that saith unto me, Lord, Lord, shall enter into the kingdom of heaven; but he that doeth the will of my Father which is in heaven" (Matthew 7:21). And so it was with Constantine. Eusebius, Constantine's friend, wrote that he "governed his empire in a godly manner for more than thirty years." Eusebius did not mention that Constantine had his son, his second wife, and his nephew all executed. Constantine was a good politician, but not a Christian.

When death approached, Constantine was baptized, thinking, as many people did in his time, that baptism washed away

---

5 Durant, p. 660.

all the sins he had committed up to that point, and it was good to put it off as long as possible.

What legacy did Constantine leave?

In any Christian's mind, the Edict of Milan stands out. Think of the great relief when persecution lifted and Christians could breathe freely again. Indeed, the Bible tells us to pray "that we may lead a quiet and peaceable life in all godliness and honesty" (1 Timothy 2:2), so it could be well said that the Edict of Milan was an answer to prayer.

The tragedy of it all was this: now that it was permissible and even popular to be a Christian, many people flooded into the church who had no business there. Ungodly people were converting the church faster than the church was converting them. Christianity was now so-called Christianity. Indeed, under a later emperor, Theodosius, Christianity became compulsory. The church, once the persecuted, had now become the persecutor.

One more item of interest: Constantine renamed the ancient city of Byzantium, calling it Constantinople after himself. That name lasted for many centuries and was not changed until AD 1930, when the government of Turkey changed its name to Istanbul.

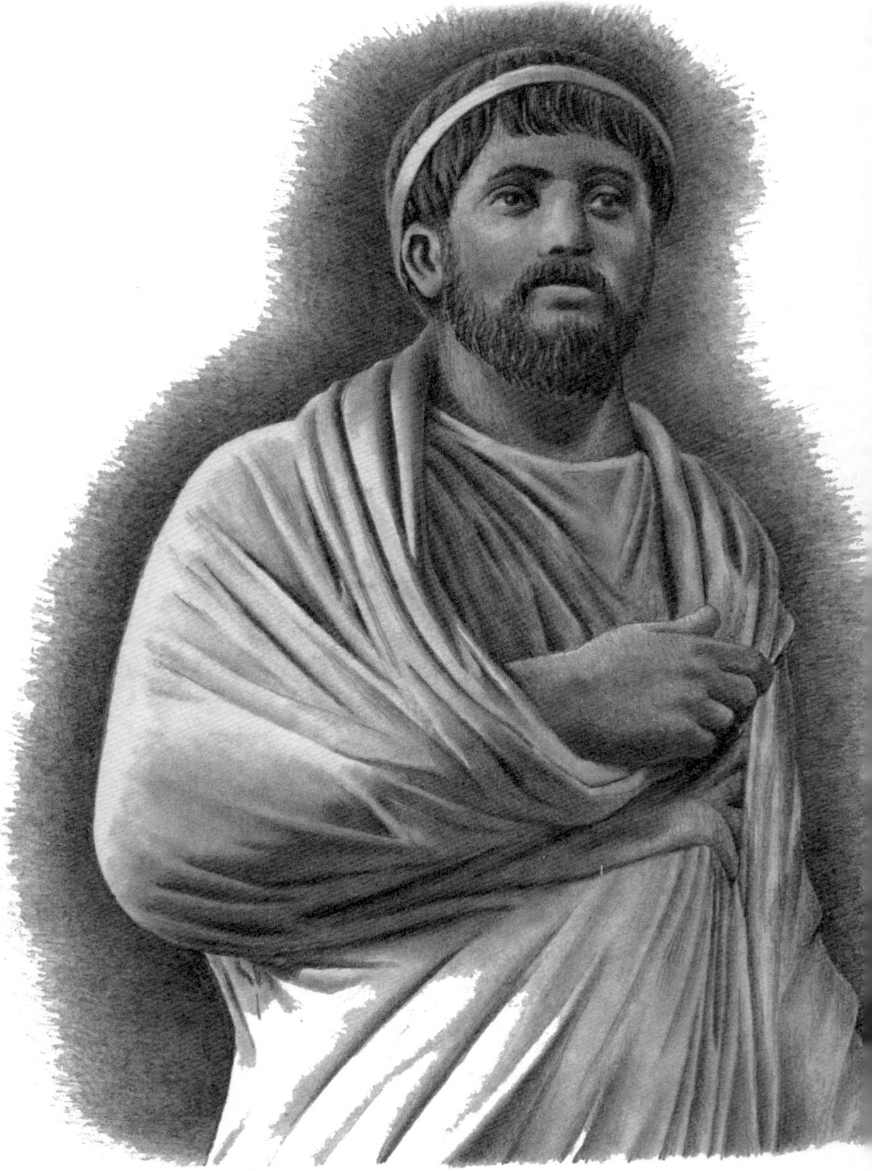

AUGUSTINE

NEW ERRORS FOR OLD HERESIES

(AD 354–430)

Not counting the apostles, which church leader has influenced people's thinking most, right down to the present day? Many students of history say it was Aurelius Augustine.

Augustine was born in northern Africa. He had a hot-tempered, ungodly father, but he also had a pious, praying mother named Monica. His parents saw that he was bright and tried to provide good schooling for him. However, instead of studying, Augustine sometimes chose to play. When he grew up, he bitterly regretted that he had never learned Greek. He wished he could read the Greek New Testament for himself.

When Augustine was sixteen or seventeen, his parents sent him to Carthage to continue his studies. His mother warned him to keep himself pure from the sins of the city, but when he arrived, he made friends with ungodly people and soon plunged deeply into sin. He was proud of it and sometimes bragged to his friends of sins he had never committed.

At age twenty-nine, Augustine decided to move to Rome. His mother begged him not to go, and then pled that he would at least take her with him. He pretended to agree, but slipped away while she was praying and sailed across the Mediterranean. His heartbroken mother, however, continued to pray for him. A friend encouraged her, "The son of so many prayers cannot be lost." Augustine himself sensed his sinfulness. "Give me purity," he prayed, "but not yet!"

Some time later, after Augustine moved to Milan, his mother found him and encouraged him to go hear the famous preacher Ambrose. Augustine was interested in rhetoric (speechmaking). In fact, he was more interested in Ambrose's hand gestures than in what Ambrose had to say. Still, as Augustine listened, something of the Gospel message slipped into his mind and influenced his thinking.

His struggles continued. The old philosophies he had studied no longer satisfied him, and the stories of Jesus appealed to him. But the true Christian life seemed to be out of his reach. Finally in frustration, he prayed, "How long? How long? Tomorrow, and again tomorrow? Why not today? Why not now? Why not in this hour put an end to my shame?"

In the quiet of his garden, he seemed to hear a voice in his heart—or was it a neighbor child singing? "Take up and read, take up and read." He reached for his copy of Romans and read, "Not in rioting and drunkenness, not in chambering and wantonness, not in strife and envying. But put ye on the Lord Jesus Christ, and make not provision for the flesh, to fulfil the lusts thereof."

... New Errors for Old Heresies

Augustine decided this was the moment to make a clean break with sin and commit his life to Jesus Christ. He was finally baptized at age thirty-three as his mother joyfully watched.

Was the struggle over? No. Once he met a woman with whom he had sinned, but he kept on walking. She called after him, "Augustine, it is I!" He replied, still hurrying along, "But it is not I!"

Moving back to northern Africa, Augustine lived a simple life with friends, praying and studying. Others followed his lifestyle until it became known as the Augustinian Order. It is the oldest of the Roman Catholic orders.

The bishop of the city of Hippo wanted help, so Augustine came to do his part. A few years later, Augustine himself was ordained bishop, even though he would have much preferred to stay living quietly in a monastery. By his own description, he was small and sickly. But he soon proved himself to be a very capable bishop. He worked hard and wrote many letters. His influence spread far.

Heresies were threatening the church. One such heresy was being preached by Pelagius, an English monk. Pelagius preached practical, victorious Christian living, which was good. But then he went so far as to preach that if you are good enough, you do not need God to save you. He should have added, "Let's cross that bridge when we come to it," because no one is ever that good. "For all have sinned, and come short of the glory of God" (Romans 3:23).

Augustine pointed out Pelagius's errors, but then he steered for the ditch on the other side of the road. He argued that absolutely no strength to do good can be found in ourselves. This

Augustine . . .

is the doctrine of total depravity. The more he thought about this, the more one link of thought led logically to another until Augustine had built a whole set of doctrines. Unfortunately, they were all false! Here are his five main points.

1. No one can do anything to save himself, not even respond to the call of God. God does it all.
2. God chooses (elects) certain people to be saved, regardless of any choices they make themselves.
3. Christ did not die for all. He died only for those people God intended to save.
4. If God chooses to save you, you cannot help but be saved.
5. A saint will not and cannot fall away from the faith.

Instead of this, we believe that the Almighty God, who does as He pleases, has been pleased to give us humans a choice. We may choose to serve or not to serve Him, but we may not choose the consequences of our choices.

Augustine promoted other errors as well. He taught that babies who die unbaptized are lost. He taught that God did not create the earth in a literal six days, but rather created a kind of basic mixture out of which everything finally developed. He believed that anyone who died outside the Roman Catholic Church was lost. He taught that Christians may fight in a war if the war is just and if they have a loving attitude toward their enemies.

Augustine had once taught that in dealing with heretics, "we must fight only by arguments." But later he changed his mind.

... New Errors for Old Heresies

He thought that since Jesus had taught, "Compel them to come in" (Luke 14:23), people might need to be forced into the church, using outright persecution if necessary. In the centuries that followed, church leaders took Augustine all too seriously, and many so-called heretics were imprisoned, tortured, drowned, and burned at the stake.

When Vandals invaded Italy and ransacked Rome, Augustine faced a great challenge. People were asking, "What kind of God is it that lets heathen people invade Rome, a great center of Christianity?" Some people argued that Christianity itself had brought tragedy upon Rome and that the best thing to do now was go back to the old Roman gods. In response, Augustine wrote a huge book called *The City of God*. He pointed out that Rome had been sacked, not because it had become Christian, but because it was not nearly Christian *enough*. He also argued that no earthly city, even Rome, is really God's city. The city of God is the church—God's people. This is true, but popes later took this to mean that church leaders should hold the real power in the world. For a time during the Middle Ages, they claimed more authority than kings themselves.

When the Vandals besieged Hippo, the city where Augustine lived, Augustine was an old man. He encouraged the starving people of his city with prayers and sermons, but three months after the siege began, he died. His epitaph, which he had composed for himself, read, "What makes the heart of the Christian heavy? The fact that he is a pilgrim, and longs for his own country."

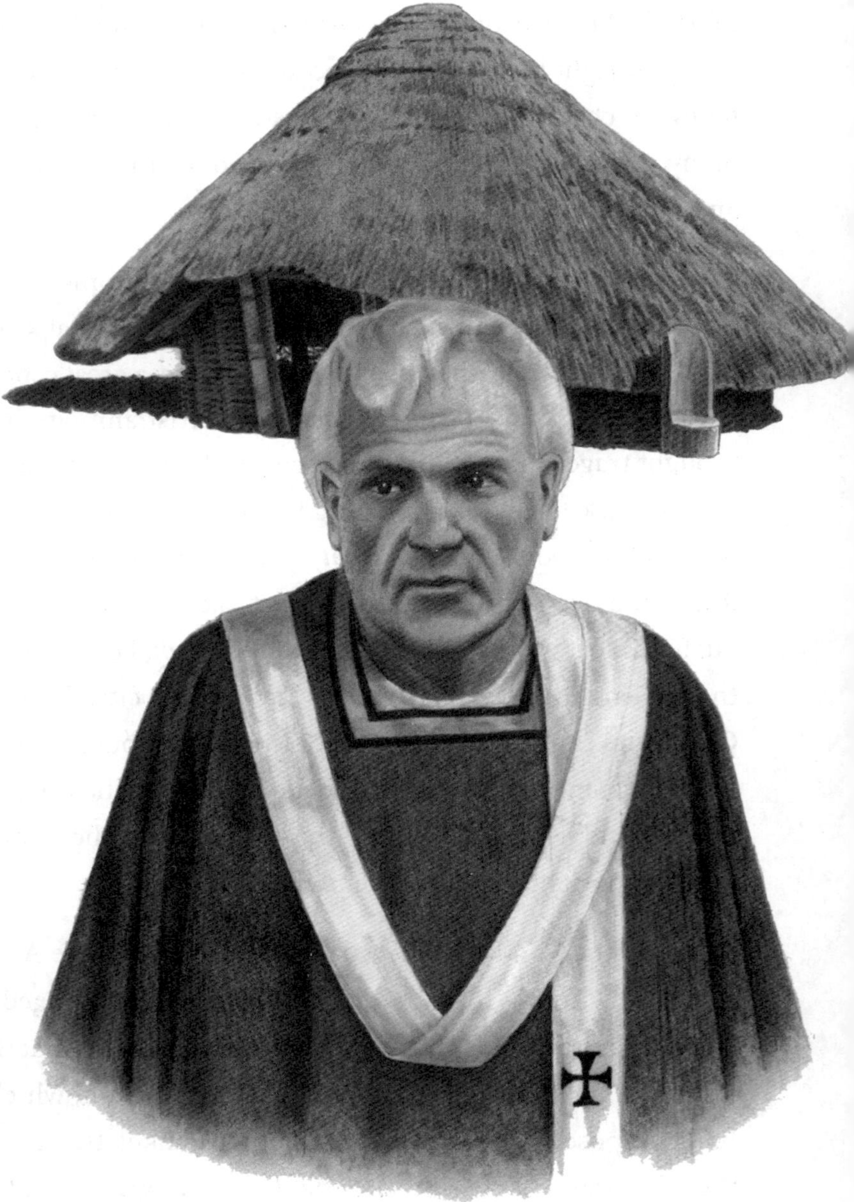

Patrick

"Apostle" to Ireland

(AD 385–461)

Ireland is called the Emerald Isle because it is green like an emerald. Of course the reason for the green is the abundant rain. The sky is often gray, and mists hang over the hills.

A few hundred years after Christ, the people who lived in Ireland were called Celts. They dressed in bright colors, loved to entertain company, and enjoyed festivals. But their religion held them in fear. They sacrificed to hundreds of gods whom they did not love and who did not love them. On their New Year's Eve, they cowered behind closed doors, leaving food outside for the spirits of the dead, who they thought roamed the country on that night. Their priests and judges, called Druids, led the people in superstitious ceremonies.

The Celts were quick to laugh but also quick to lose their temper. They held grudges and raided each other's territories.

Patrick . . .

They fought each other more than they fought foreigners, but they did find time to raid the English coast. Among many things they carried away, they took slaves.

One time their English captives included a sixteen-year-old lad named Patrick. Patrick's father was a Catholic deacon, while his grandfather had been a Catholic priest. His new captors made him a shepherd. It was a rough life, especially in winter, when Ireland's damp chill crept into his bones as he worked. Year after year, as he worked, he prayed urgently that God would deliver him and let him return to England. Year after year, even though he had no Bible to read, he drew closer to the Lord and understood Him better. Patrick learned to know Gaelic, the language of the people, and he also learned their customs.

After six years of unceasing prayer, Patrick received dreams directing him to go to the eastern shore of Ireland and meet a ship there. Patrick fled, hiking for days until he reached the coast. There, sure enough, was a ship. The sailors took him on board, but then, to Patrick's shock, they made him a slave! What had happened to the Lord's promise to get him back to England? In another dream, the Lord reassured him that this captivity would only last for two months. Soon he would be on his way home. The sailors finally let him go, but he was in a strange land, which some people think is now called France.

When he finally reached home and family and was thinking about where to take his life from there, he received yet another dream. This one directed him to go back to the Irish people, bringing them the Gospel! After this jolt to his thinking, Patrick told his family and friends. They tried to persuade him that the Lord wanted him to stay among them. Why go back to a land he had prayed for years to escape from? His church leaders dragged their feet too, pointing out that he had much to learn about the Bible and church doctrine. "You are not yet ready to be a missionary," they said.

So Patrick prayed again—this time for twenty-five years! In the meantime, he studied hard and became a presbyter (church leader). At last the church consented to ordain him a bishop for Ireland, and soon afterward, he set sail with a few companions.

Once again, life in Ireland was tough. Preaching in rain or trying to sleep in cold shelters, Patrick shivered, not only from the weather, but also sometimes from illness. But the difficulties did not take him by surprise. His old memories of the damp, chilly weather fortified him now. And his knowledge of Gaelic and of Irish customs served as a great help to him.

People responded to this fearless preacher who understood their language so well. Patrick and his helpers baptized thousands of people, ordained leaders among them, and baptized thousands more. Christianity had come to Ireland.

Patrick not only preached, he also taught practical Christian living. He disciplined or even excommunicated members who were not living godly lives or who had not completely turned away from their old ways of worshiping.

To this day, people celebrate St. Patrick's Day on March 17th, the day he died. They wear something green to commemorate the day. Some cities hold parades. Catholics today venerate Patrick as a saint, and consider him to have done much to advance Catholicism.

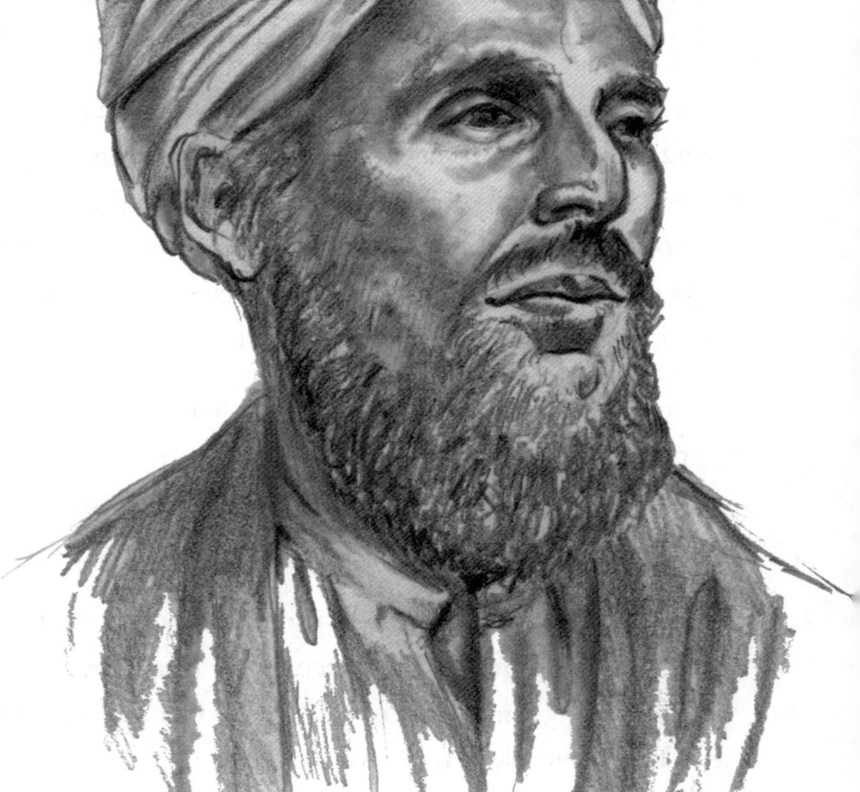

Muhammed

The Birth of Islam

(AD 570–632)

Robes and turbans are not a bad idea in a desert where the sun shines dazzlingly bright and the hot winds blow stinging sand. Many centuries ago in Arabia, most people in the sparsely-populated desert lived the way some of them still live today—as Bedouin nomads, moving their flocks from pasture to pasture to keep from overgrazing one area.

In this land once lived a sensitive young fellow named Muhammed. He had the chance to talk to Christians and Jews and find out what they believed. Rather than simply accepting everything they said, he thought about it. In their religions, he found much to admire—certainly much more than in the religions of the many idol worshipers around him. However, he believed there should be a new religion that fit his fellow Arabs better than anything the Christians or Jews had to offer.

Muhammed...

When Muhammed was twenty-five, he married a forty-year-old widow who became his close friend and gave him much encouragement. While married to her, he had a strange dream. It seemed to him that the angel Gabriel came to him and said, "Read!" But Muhammed had never learned to read, and he told the angel so. Gabriel pinned him down frighteningly hard and insisted, "Read!" Suddenly, in his dream, Muhammed could read what Gabriel asked him to read. "And I awoke from my sleep, and it was as if these words were written on my heart."

When Muhammed told his wife about this strange vision, she believed it was a real visitation from an angel and assured him he was a prophet. Muhammed was slow to put himself forward, but as he gained confidence, he began to share his vision of a new faith with others. He especially condemned the idol worship he saw all around him.

This aroused the anger of many people in his hometown of Mecca. Muhammed fled for his life to a nearby cave, and then by night toward another town, Medina, two hundred miles away. When he arrived, friends gave him a warm welcome. Medina, with its farms and orchards, was a more pleasant town than the desert-like Mecca. Muhammed's flight from Mecca to Medina in AD 622 has been made very famous. It is called the Hegira, and Muslims date their calendars from that time.

The people of Medina soon had a problem. Hundreds of people had flooded into the town, and there were too many mouths to feed. Where to find food? Muhammed solved the problem in the Arab fashion typical for those days. He staged

... The Birth of Islam

raids on camel caravans that traveled near Medina. The merchants of Mecca, who depended on trade, were outraged when various frightened, injured travelers showed up and told how they had been robbed. More than once the people of Mecca raised small armies against Muhammed, but they could never quite defeat him. The time came when Muhammed rode triumphantly into Mecca and took command of it.

Muhammed and his followers continued to expand their control over neighboring territories. Muhammed assured his soldiers that he would share the spoils with them if they won. And if they were killed, that was best of all; would they not go straight to paradise? Although Muhammed lived only ten years after his flight to Medina, his followers boldly carried on what they called jihad—holy war. The more lands they conquered, the more frightened their enemies became. When they heard that the followers of Muhammed were coming, many thought it might be best to surrender and pay whatever taxes they had to pay.

Along with the Muslim conquerors came their religion, which was basically the same religion we see Muslims observing today. Their holy book is the Koran, which is a little shorter than the New Testament. Many Muslims memorize it, believing there is virtue in the very words themselves.

Muslims believe in what they call the Five Pillars: (1) Acceptance of God. Every day a Muslim must say, "There is no god but Allah, and Muhammed is his prophet." *Allah* simply means "God." (2) Prayer. A devout Muslim prays memorized prayers five times a day. (3) Almsgiving. (4) Fasting. During the month

Muhammed... The Birth of Islam

of Ramadan, Muslims are not supposed to eat or drink during daylight hours. They may eat after night falls. (5) Pilgrimage to Mecca. Every good Muslim is expected to travel to Mecca at least once during his lifetime.

Muhammed's movement has spread around the world. Today Muslims are strong in countries where, fifty years ago, they were few. England, for instance, has many Muslims, and their numbers are growing in countries like America as well.

How does Islam compare to Christianity? It is a great religion—in the sense that it is widespread and millions of people believe in it. But it is not a peaceful religion like Christianity. It is true that many so-called Christians fight among themselves and even go to war, but they have to violate the teachings of Christ to do it. In the case of Islam, it is the other way around. Many Muslims are pleasant and peaceful as they relate to their neighbors, but the fact remains that the founder of their religion was violent, and many Muslims today follow his example.

Still, Muslims are people. What does an apricot taste like to a Muslim? Probably much the same as it does to you and me. What remedy for sin does he need? The blood of Jesus Christ, just as we do.

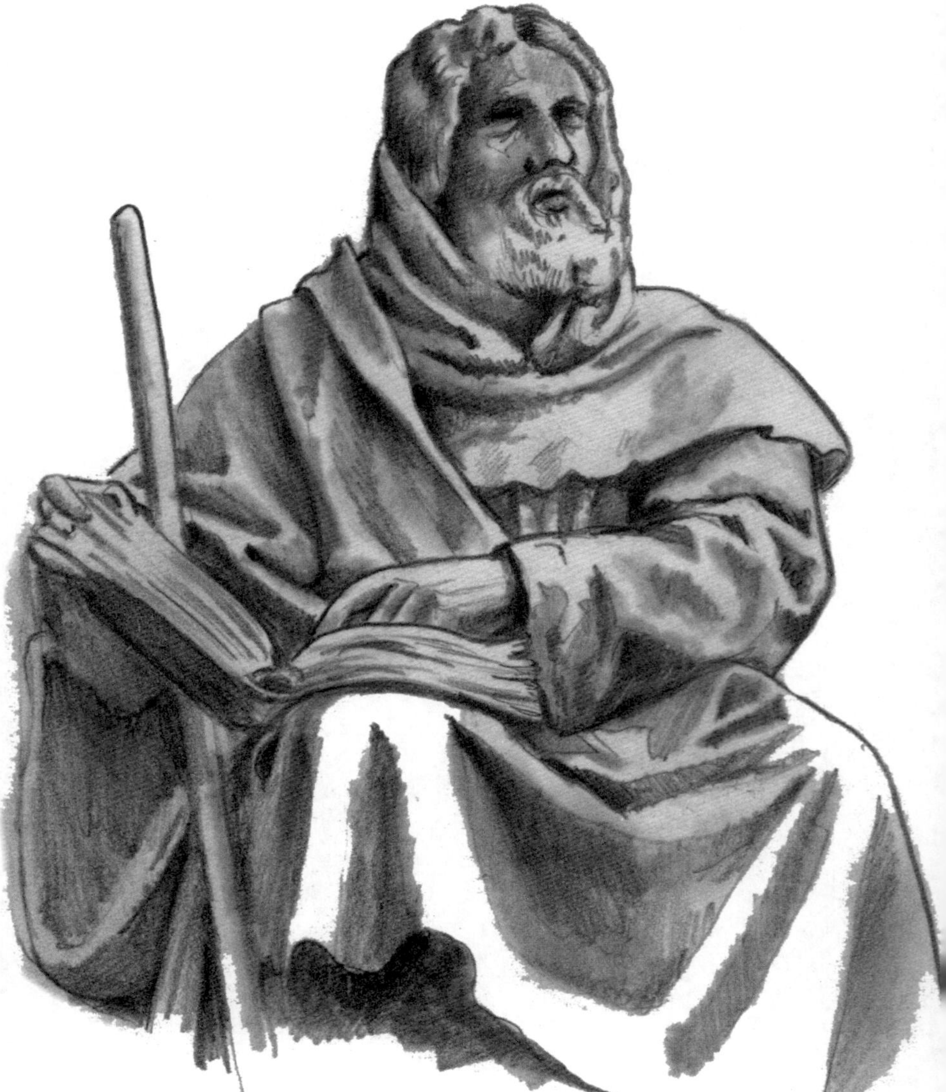

PETER WALDO

THE WALDENSIANS

(AD ?–1217)

On a summer day in Lyons, France, around 1160, several men stood together talking. Suddenly one of the men slumped to the ground and died. Another man in the group, a well-to-do businessman named Peter Waldo, was much sobered. He reflected on the fact that life is uncertain and short, and he wondered how he could best spend the remaining years of his own life.

Peter brought his questions to a priest, who pointed out the words of Jesus to the rich young ruler: "If thou wilt be perfect, go and sell that thou hast, and give to the poor, and thou shalt have treasure in heaven: and come and follow me" (Matthew 19:21). Peter applied this to himself. After providing for his wife and children, he began to give away his goods. Wearing simple clothes such as any poor man might wear, he walked here and there, preaching the Gospel and living on whatever people gave

Peter Waldo . . .

him. It appears that Peter also used his means to have the Bible translated into the language of southern France. He studied the Bible in his own tongue and shared what he learned with other people. Other men joined Peter, who sent them out two by two, as Jesus had done. Because they followed Peter's simple example, they became known as the "Poor Men of Lyons."

At first, the Catholic Church of that time did not mind these men's activities. They were even allowed to read the Bible to the people during services. But when the group of traveling preachers grew, the local bishop pointed out to Peter that he and his men did not have a license to preach. So Peter paid a visit to the pope, who gave him a license, on one condition—they must preach only where the local church leaders approved. Soon Peter gave up trying to follow the pope's direction. Had not God called His disciples to preach everywhere?

Church leaders felt threatened by the wandering preachers. Since they knew all too well that there were spiritual needs in their own church, they began a group of Poor Catholics who also traveled about doing good. They were called friars (brothers). St. Francis founded the Franciscans (gray friars) in 1208; St. Dominic founded the Dominicans (black friars) in 1215. These Catholic orders, along with others, helped some people to stay within the Catholic Church.

As Peter and his followers continued to study the Bible, they found no Scriptural support for various doctrines they had been taught. Did people suffer after they died, in a place called purgatory, to prepare them to enter heaven? No. Should one

... The Waldensians

pray to the saints? No. Did it do any good to pray for the dead? No. Over many past years, quite a few other people had been raising similar objections. Peter Waldo and his followers gave an enormous boost to the dissenters.

The Waldenses, or Waldensians, as Peter Waldo's followers were called, were among the more sensible of the dissenters. Other people, such as the Albigenses, believed that everything material is somehow evil, and that only that which is spiritual is good. The Waldenses did not agree with this; the Bible says that "God saw every thing that he had made, and, behold, it was very good" (Genesis 1:31).

When fierce persecution finally arose, the Catholic Church did not always make a difference between the Albigenses and the Waldenses. They burned both at the stake. The Waldenses fled to mountain valleys in the Alps where they could quietly live their faith. For hundreds of years, they kept the Gospel light glowing.

Reinerius, a Dominican friar, paid the Waldenses some compliments, without meaning to, in his following description of them:

> "Among all the sects that ever were and still are, there is none more pernicious [harmful] ... than the sect of the Lyonists [Waldenses], and this for three reasons. "*Firstly*, because it is the most ancient; for some say that it has existed from the time of Sylvester; others say, from the time of the apostles.

"*Secondly*, because it is more general [widespread] than other sects; for there is no country where this sect is not found.

"*Thirdly*, because, whereas all other sects, by their abominable blasphemies against God, cause those who hear them, to loathe their belief, this sect, on the other hand, has a great semblance of godliness, because they lead a godly life before men, have a true belief in all things concerning God, and hold correct views in regard to all the twelve articles of faith; only they condemn the Roman church and the clergy, in which the unlearned too readily credit them."[6]

During the 1500s, the Waldenses came in contact with Protestant leaders who persuaded them to lay aside many of their beliefs. After that, it was the Anabaptists who carried on the old torch. But many people—thousands, in fact—still call themselves Waldenses and live in Europe and the Americas.

---

[6] Thieleman J. van Braght, *Martyrs Mirror*, trans. Joseph F. Sohm (Scottdale, PA: Herald Press, 1972), p. 283.

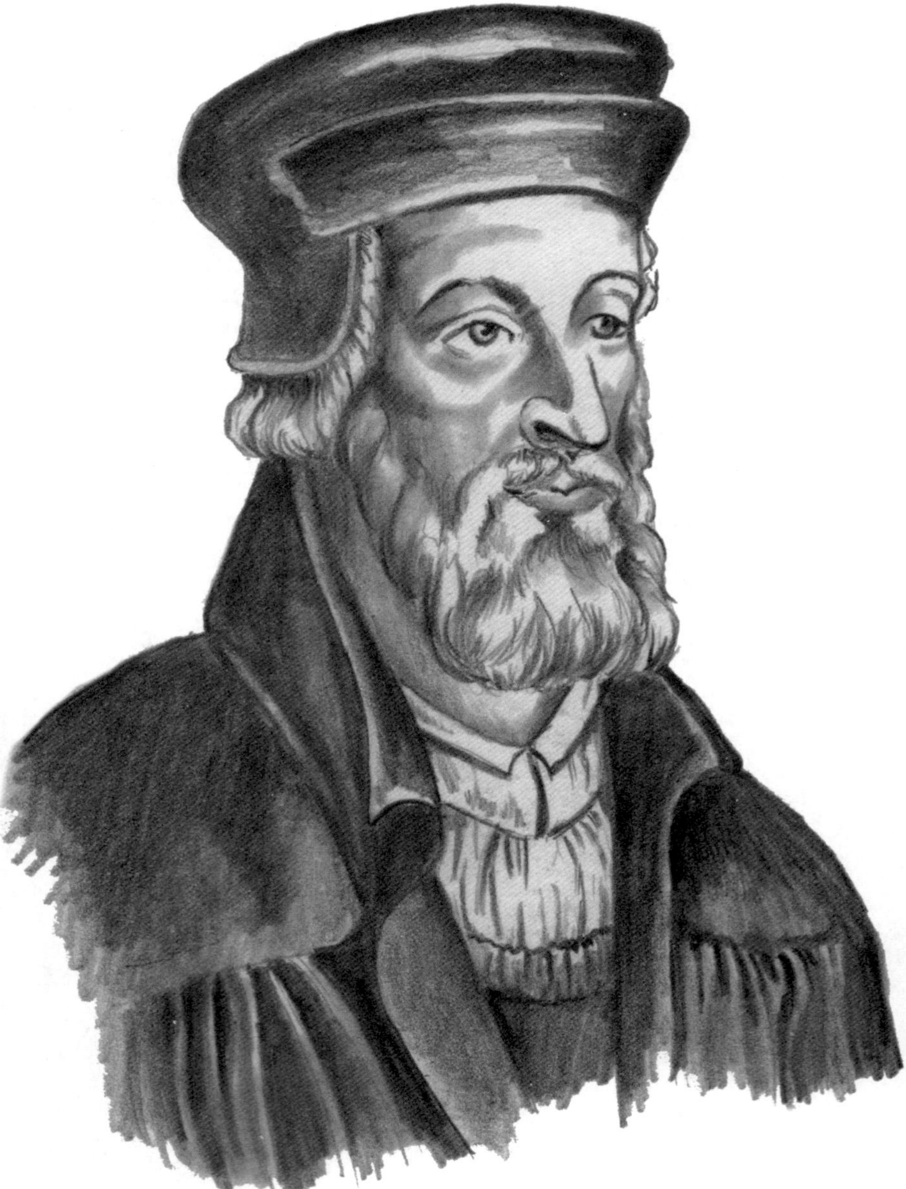

John Wycliffe

Morning Star of the Reformation

(AD 1328?–1384)

It is hard for us, who live in the twenty-first century, to imagine what a trip across England was like during the 1300s. England's roads were dusty in summer and muddy in winter, and bandits lurked at unexpected corners. Since travel was slow, difficult, and dangerous, most people never ventured far from home and rarely talked to someone from even a dozen miles away. This meant that England was full of little pockets of people who talked differently from each other. In fact, England had nearly two hundred different dialects. Travel only a dozen miles, and you might not be able to understand the people's language.

Three-fourths of the people were peasants (poor farmers), and half of the peasants were serfs (near-slaves). Towns were crammed with rickety houses that quickly burned when a small fire got out of control. People tossed garbage onto the streets.

John Wycliffe...

Rats scurried here and there, carrying disease. During the 1300s and 1400s, the Black Plague struck England again and again, killing about a third of the people.

What was available to read in the 1300s? Nothing—at least, nothing printed. This was still a hundred years before Johann Gutenberg set up the first printing press. Books were handwritten manuscripts to be found in libraries, colleges, and monasteries.

However, not everyone was ignorant. Some people knew Greek or Hebrew and could read the Bible in the original languages. Quite a few people knew Latin, the language of learning at that time. John Wycliffe, a teacher at Oxford University, had access to the Bible and spent much time reading it. To him, the key to all truth was the Bible. He had a penetrating mind, and when he made discoveries in the Bible, he said out loud what he thought about them.

The Jesus whom John Wycliffe found in the Bible was quite different from the church leaders that John saw in his own day. Jesus, he said, was a lowly man; the pope lived like a king. Jesus' disciples lived very simple lives, more like the peasants of England than like the church leaders, who wore silk, jingled gold in their purses, and rode in fine carriages. John did not like to see the bishop ride up to a church door and collect a heavy offering so he could continue to live in luxury while the common people patiently sacrificed their meager earnings to the church.

John said, moreover, that the church was too worldly and too loose with sin. He said the church was wrong to think people could pay their way to heaven rather than letting God save them, or to let people believe that they could make up for a bad life by taking the bread and wine of the Mass.

For his blunt talk and unpopular opinions, John lost friends and made enemies. Once when he was deathly ill, some churchmen came to his bedside and pointedly told him he would go to hell if he did not recant. That was just the shot in the arm he needed—he became so indignant that he recovered!

The most powerful thing John did was to put into people's hands the very Book he had been reading. He and his helpers began to translate the New Testament into English. It would have been most accurate to translate straight from Greek, but since John and his helpers could not do that, they did the next best thing—they translated from Latin. Other scholars began to translate the Old Testament.

John and his helpers did not wait until the whole Bible was translated before they began handing it around. As soon as a part was finished, they enthusiastically copied and recopied it and tried to get it into the hands of as many people as possible.

But so many people could not read! How could they get the message? There was only one answer. Preachers would have to walk to various communities and read to the people. Poor preachers, that is—not the wandering friars of those days, but sincere men who wore simple rust-brown robes, broad-brimmed hats, and sandals—men content to carry with them not much more than walking sticks and Bibles.

John Wycliffe . . .

Although orthodox churchmen scorned the poor preachers as "Lollards" (babblers), the common people loved them. As the Lollards read portions of Scripture to them, the people memorized the passages. And more than just the common people sat up and took notice. It appears that some priests, bishops, and other churchmen quietly made copies of their own. Some of those handwritten copies still exist today.

The Lollards pointed out various errors in the church of their day. They did not believe that priests should be required to remain unmarried, that the bread and wine of the Mass became the actual body and blood of Jesus Christ, that images should be adored, that it did any good to pray for the dead, that it was necessary to confess sins to priests, or that anyone should pray to saints. They said that taking part in war is wrong. They taught that everyone should live simply. They would not swear oaths, saying instead, "I am sure."

But some churchmen and government leaders worried that as the peasants listened to Wycliffe's ideas, so different from what the church had taught them, they would finally revolt against both church and government. Indeed, there came a time when many peasants did revolt, breaking into homes and offices, smashing costly items, destroying records, and killing men they considered enemies of the common people. In the end, their leader was killed and the revolt subsided. Government officials blamed the Lollards, although Lollards in general were peaceable people who did not believe in revolt.

More than once, officials gathered as many pieces of English Scripture as they could and burned them. They hunted down the Lollards and executed some of them. Lord Cobham, who had helped to supply money for Wycliffe's work, testified before his questioners, "Before God and man, I profess solemnly here that I never abstained from sin until I knew Wycliffe, whom ye so much disdain." Despite his testimony, the church had Lord Cobham burned.

Nevertheless, John Wycliffe's influence could not be stopped. And his translation of the Bible produced an interesting side benefit. As his Bible spread across England, people of various dialects began to imitate the language they found in the Bible they were reading. This was a great advantage, because then they began to talk more like each other. The next time the Bible was translated into English, more people would understand it from the start.

Even after Wycliffe finally died, the church did not forgive him. In 1415, some thirty years after his death, the Council of Constance declared that not only should his books be burned but his body should be exhumed and burned as well. Although Wycliffe's ashes were scattered into a river and never seen again, John Wycliffe has long been known as the Morning Star of the Reformation.

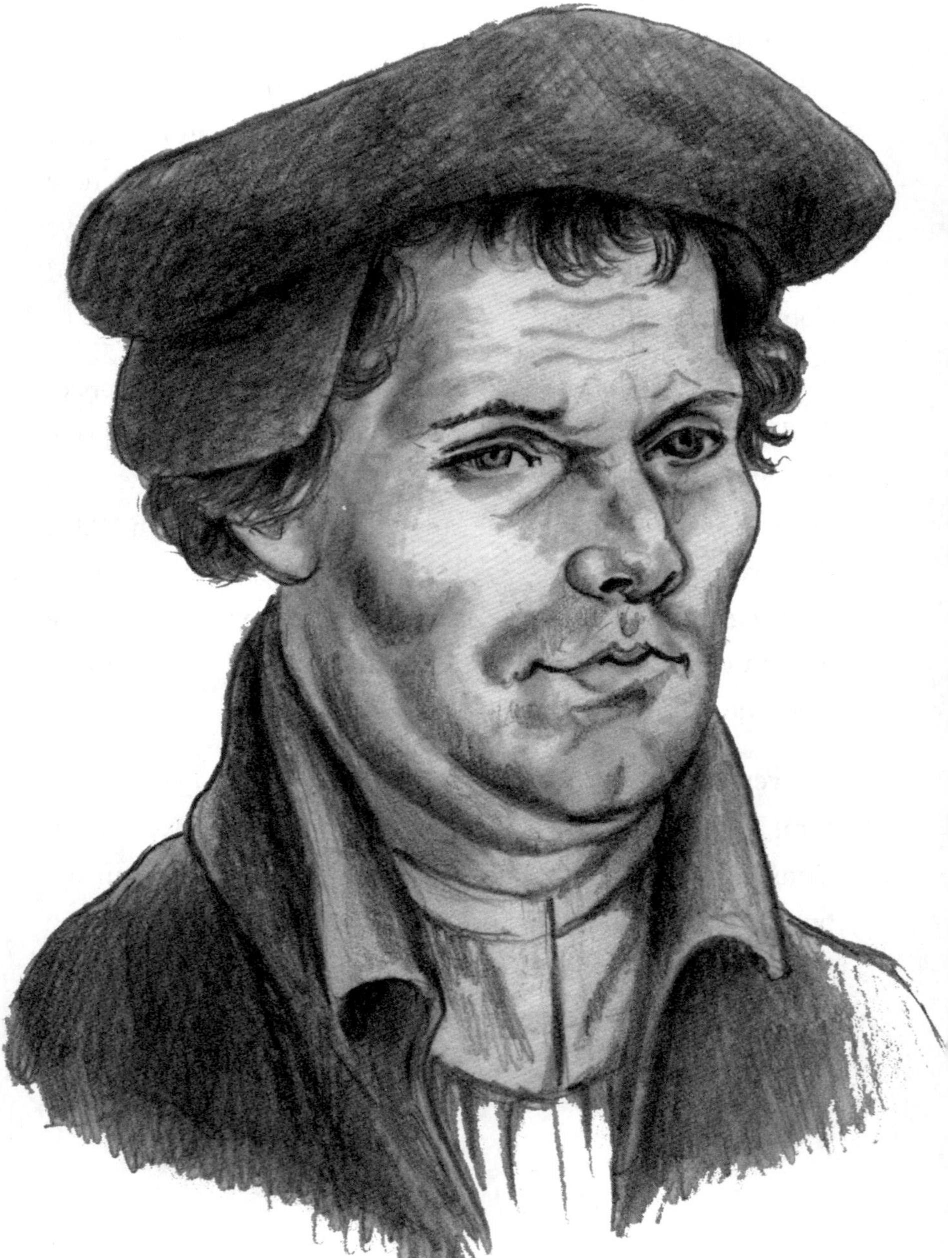

Martin Luther

The Reformation Begins in Germany

(AD 1483–1546)

Renaissance is pronounced REN · uh · szahns. It refers to the long period of time when Europe crept out of the Middle Ages into the time of the Reformation. During the Renaissance, people discussed exciting new ideas. They also rediscovered old ideas that were new to them. Scholars pored over musty manuscripts and pondered what the ancient Greeks had said. Some of them spent time with the Bible. The Bible became available to more people after the mid-1400s, when Johann Gutenberg invented the moveable-type printing press.

As thinkers entertained new ideas, they began to question ideas that they had long thought to be correct. Some men became quite outspoken as they expressed their doubts. One such man was Desiderius Erasmus. In those days, the Catholic Church sold relics to its people—things like a lock of a saint's hair, or maybe even one of his bones. The relics were supposed to bring God's blessing, perhaps even miraculous answers to prayer, to whoever possessed them. One such relic was a piece of Christ's cross. How many pieces there were! Erasmus grumbled that if all the supposed pieces were brought together, they would fill a good-sized ship. Although he never left the Catholic Church, it is said that "Erasmus laid the egg that Luther hatched."

Martin Luther was born in Germany, the son of a hard-working miner. Martin's father, seeing how bright he was, sent him to law school. But one day as Martin was walking through the forest, a thunderstorm crashed over him and lightning struck so near that he cried out, "St. Ann! Spare me, and I will become a monk." Despite his father's disappointment and anger, Martin left the study of law and enrolled in a monastery.

As Martin delved into his studies, he became more and more troubled at the thought of his own sinfulness. No matter how he prayed, fasted, studied, or stayed up at night, he felt condemned before God. Finally, a Bible verse that he had read before stood out to him in a new way. "The just shall live by faith" (Romans 1:17). It dawned on him then that his trust in the Lord's work—not his own works—opened the door for God to justify him. Martin's discovery transformed his life and caused him to feel that he had found peace.

Alas, many other people had not discovered peace. Many church members worked hard to win their salvation, or paid much. Paying money for forgiveness of sin became quite popular. It was easy, at least for people who had money, and it paid for

... The Reformation Begins in Germany

the church's expenses. One of the most flagrant examples was that of Tetzel, a friar who sold indulgences. These, he said, were pardons from the pope for sins the people committed. One could even buy indulgences for sins he had not yet committed. And, yes, the indulgences worked for people who had already died. This sounded like wonderful news, for the Catholics believed that after a person died, he spent time in the flames of purgatory, suffering for any sins still unpardoned. Tetzel went so far as to say in effect, "When the coin in the coffer rings, the soul from purgatory springs."

To Luther, who had come to feel that pardon from God is free through Christ, who has already paid it all, this was outrageous. So he wrote a list of arguments against Tetzel's trade, and added some dry comments about the way the Catholic Church was run. Luther had an idea what was going on in the church. He had even made a trip to Rome and had learned that indulgences were only one of various abuses in the church. By the time Luther was finished writing, he had ninety-five arguments.

In 1517, the day before All Saints' Day (modern Halloween), Luther took his Ninety-Five Theses to the church door at his hometown of Wittenberg, Germany, and nailed them up there for everyone to see. He wrote his arguments in Latin, and was surprised when some of his readers translated them into German and published them far and wide. Luther was still learning about the power of the printing press.

Luther's dangerous words came to the ears of the pope, Leo X. When Leo had become pope, he had said, "God has given us the papacy. Let us enjoy it." He obviously saw life from a different perspective than Luther. After various efforts to bring Luther to his senses, the pope asked Emperor Charles V and his counselors to meet with Luther. This meeting took place at Worms, in Germany. By this time, Luther was considered an outlaw, so he was promised a safe-conduct (a guarantee that he would not be arrested on the trip) to and from Worms. When Luther came, he was shown a pile of books and was asked two questions. "Did you write these? And do you recant their contents?"

Of course Luther had written them, and he said so. As to the second question, he asked for a day to think over his answer. On the following day, standing before the council again, he admitted that he had not said everything just right. But when pressed, he said some of the most famous words in history (perhaps with the help of printers who later polished his words). "Here I stand. I can do no other. God help me! Amen."

Luther knew that his words would get him into big trouble. As soon as his safe-conduct ended, perhaps even before that, officers would be looking for him. John Hus, a follower of Wycliffe, had been offered a safe-conduct to Geneva, only to be arrested and burned. Indeed, as Luther traveled homeward, suddenly masked horsemen appeared from nowhere, snatched Luther from the cart he was riding in, and galloped off. Luther's friends were appalled. Luther's career was over!

But Luther knew better, or soon did. His friend Elector Frederick had made the incident look like a kidnapping so that Luther's enemies would not look for him. The Elector found a

... The Reformation Begins in Germany

home for Luther in a castle of his at Wartburg. Luther's room was not cozy, but at least it was safe and quiet. Luther grew a beard, called himself "George," and got busy writing. One of his major projects was a translation of the New Testament into German. The work went fast, and Luther published the German New Testament the following year.

The Old Testament was bigger and more difficult, and Luther took nearly a dozen years to complete it. He wanted the Bible to be written in the language of the common Germans, so he took time to talk to the common people. He visited butcher shops to find out what terms to use when speaking of Old Testament sacrifices. He talked to children at play. Still, the work was very slow and difficult. Luther complained that translating from Hebrew into German was like trying to teach a nightingale to imitate a cuckoo. Nevertheless, the German Bible he produced was widely accepted for hundreds of years.

However, in prefaces he wrote for each of the New Testament books, Luther taught some ideas of his own. Some of these ideas were good, and some were not. The Bible says "justified by faith," but Luther said "justified by faith only." By weakening the place of works in Christian experience, he overlooked an important truth: faith works! (Ephesians 2:8–10).

The lives of Luther's followers vividly illustrated that Luther had failed to teach them some basics. Since they were saved by faith only, they could (they thought) live as sinfully as common Catholics and not even need to pay for indulgences. Luther was dismayed at his people's sinfulness, admitting, "Peasants, citizens, nobles, all are more covetous and undisciplined than they were under the Papacy." When an Anabaptist leader, Conrad Grebel, wrote to him, challenging him on the state of affairs in his church and trying to show him a better way, Luther admitted that he was at a loss to know how to answer him.

Worst of all was the peasants' revolt. The many peasants in Germany struggled with hunger, ill health, and heavy taxes. The nobles of the time kept them oppressed with severe punishments, like cutting off a man's hands because he caught a rabbit on his own property. Luther disapproved of the oppression, and wrote in severe language what he thought of it. Learning of this, the peasants thought they had Luther's support to revolt. And why not, since Luther himself had revolted against the church? Were not the church and the government so tied together that to rebel against one was to rebel against the other?

In scattered bands, the peasants began looting, burning, and killing. At first Luther called upon both peasants and nobles to give in a little. The nobles should give the peasants more rights, and the peasants should back off their most unreasonable demands. However, when the violence continued, Luther changed his tune. He exhorted the government to "smite, slay, and stab" the peasants, and it did. Over a hundred thousand peasants were killed. Tens of thousands were left to walk the roads, homeless.

And this, people said, was Luther's fault. Luther had supported the peasants at first, but then turned traitor. Many people

. . . The Reformation Begins in Germany

turned away from the Lutheran church and became Catholics again. Others became atheists. Still others became Anabaptists.

The Radical Trio

The Swiss Brethren Forge Ahead

(AD 1525–1529)

"Radical" is usually an uncomplimentary word. But the radical reformers were called that because they were radical compared to other reformers, who should have been more radical. As the Protestant reformers shook the Catholic Church, the radical reformers shook the Protestant church.

The radical reformers came to be called the Swiss Brethren. Their leaders were Conrad Grebel, Felix Manz, and George Blaurock. Grebel was leader among the three leaders, but all had their unique part to play. All played it bravely, but briefly. Within a few years after they had founded the movement, all three were dead.

The Radical Trio...

Their story begins with the Protestant reformer, Ulrich Zwingli. What Martin Luther was to Germany, Ulrich Zwingli was to Switzerland. He, Grebel, Manz, and other friends started meetings in which they would read the Bible and comment on it. The Bible was a relatively new book to them, and they made new discoveries.

One of the things they learned was that the emblems of the bread and cup that Jesus served at the Last Supper were just that—emblems. They were not the body and blood of Jesus, as the Catholic Church said they were. They also learned that in the Bible, no infants were baptized, only believers. They discovered that other practices, such as having images in churches, did not fit the New Testament way of thinking.

After Zwingli and his followers had held meetings for a time, they began to disagree. Zwingli wanted to do away with the abuses he found in the church, but he wanted to do it in cooperation with the Zurich council. Conrad Grebel and Felix Manz, however, did not want to wait for the civil government to approve what the church was doing.

How difficult it was for many people of those days to understand separation of church and state! The church and the government had been tied together for centuries. Children were baptized into the church shortly after they were born. If people were allowed to choose whether to be baptized or not, how would that work? What if they chose the wrong church or made no choice at all? How could the government govern?

... The Swiss Brethren Forge Ahead

In October of 1523, Zwingli and his friends had a public debate with the Romanists. Some things, like disapproving of images in the church, Zwingli and his friends agreed with each other on. Upon other things, however, it became apparent that they did not agree with each other at all. At one point, Conrad Grebel said, "The one thing necessary before all else is the abolition of the Mass. Much has been said about the Mass, but none of the priests is willing to forsake this great abomination." Zwingli replied, "The Council will decide concerning the Mass." At this, Simon Stumpf, another debater, said, "Master Ulrich [Zwingli], you have not the right to leave the decision of this question to the Council. The matter is already decided; the Spirit of God decides it."[7]

The following year, George Blaurock came to Zurich to talk to Zwingli. Blaurock had been a monk, but he had become troubled by Catholic doctrines he could no longer agree with. After various discussions with Zwingli, he heard that other reformers in the area had been more thorough in their reforms than Zwingli. When Blaurock finally met Grebel and Manz, he knew he had come home.

One winter night, the brethren met in the home of Felix Manz's mother. Overwhelmed with their need to make good choices in the face of persecution, they all slipped to their knees to ask God's help and guidance. Then George Blaurock asked Conrad Grebel to baptize him. When Grebel had done so, Blaurock baptized all the rest. It was on or near January 21, 1525. The Swiss Brethren movement had officially begun.

---

[7] John Horsch, *Mennonites in Europe* (Crockett, KY: Rod and Staff Publishers, 1995), pp. 34–35.

The Radical Trio...

The three leaders did not keep their activities a secret. They preached and taught from house to house, baptized many people, and frequently observed Communion, which they called "breaking of bread." Zwingli saw the new movement as a threat. Was not the law being violated? In February, his officers imprisoned twenty-four men and women, including Grebel, Manz, and Blaurock. They were released shortly, but later imprisonments were more severe.

In the summer of 1526, Conrad Grebel died of the plague in his sister's home. Although his time of service was cut very short, he had helped to light a torch that others would carry onward.

Felix Manz's time ended the following January, when the Zurich council decided to make a public example of him. As friends and enemies watched from the shore of the Limmat River, his executioners rowed him to the middle of the river, bound him, and cast him in. But before he died, his friends and his mother shouted encouragement to him. Manz himself called out in Latin, "Into thy hand, O God, I commit my spirit." Felix Manz was the first martyr put to death by Protestants.

George Blaurock was the most outspoken of the three leaders and was sometimes called the "second Paul." At least once, he walked into a Reformed church, informed the preacher that he had come to preach, and took over the service. When the preacher returned with officers, Blaurock refused to quiet down, even when he was bodily taken out and hustled down the street. At last, in 1529, when serving in a Catholic region, he and a friend were burned at the stake.

... The Swiss Brethren Forge Ahead

How could these people be so strong as to endure such persecution so faithfully? It was not their belief or disbelief in certain doctrines that gave them courage; it was their love for the Lord. Their obedience grew out of that living relationship with Him.

Interestingly, Zwingli himself lived only until 1531. The Protestant movement had been so successful near Zurich that he hoped all Switzerland could be made Protestant. But other portions of Switzerland formed the Catholic League to work against Zwingli. After some rattling of swords, the Catholics and Protestants finally met and fought. Five hundred men from Zurich were killed, including Ulrich Zwingli.

In Zurich, where Ulrich Zwingli once preached, stands a statue on a high pedestal, showing Zwingli holding a Bible in one hand and a big sword in the other. But Grebel, Manz, and Blaurock enjoy lasting honors of their own. Imperfectly but surely, these three men paved the way for a movement that has not died to this day. Hundreds of thousands of people look back to the Swiss Brethren as their spiritual fathers.

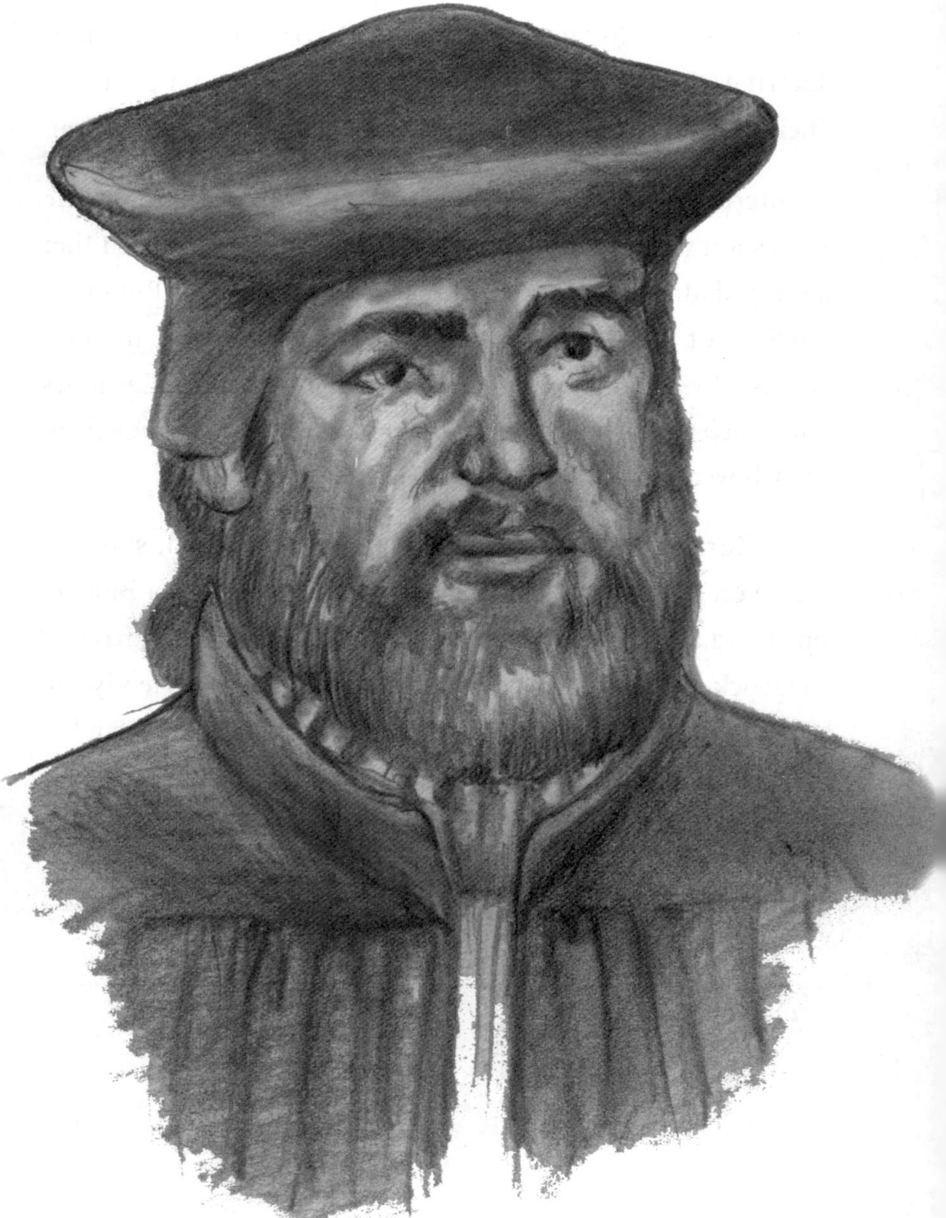

MICHAEL SATTLER

A SIGN IN THE FIRE

(AD 1495?–1527)

After Conrad Grebel and Felix Manz died, the most outstanding leader of the Swiss Brethren was Michael Sattler. However, as with the other leaders, his career was cut short. Manz had been drowned in January 1527; Sattler was burned in May.

As a young man, Sattler was a devout Catholic; in fact, he chose to become a monk. Although his fellow monks disappointed him, he himself did well within the monastery. In time he became the prior, which is the second-highest official in a monastery. However, as he read the Bible and the writings of the early church fathers, he saw more and more that there must be a better way. In 1523, he left the monastery and married.

In 1525, Sattler came to Zurich and joined the Swiss Brethren. Like other brethren, he was banished from Zurich the same year.

Michael Sattler...

Sattler decided to travel north and spent some time in southern Germany. In Strasbourg, he had a long talk with Reformed leaders. They tried to win him over, but later he wrote them a long letter explaining why he could not work with them.

In February of 1527, Sattler presided over a meeting of Swiss Brethren in Schleitheim, northern Switzerland. They agreed to write down various points that united them. The Schleitheim Confession did not cover the points on which Christians generally agree, but spoke right to the points on which the Swiss Brethren differed from the Catholics and Protestants. Some of the main points of the Confession were the following.

- ❖ Only believers should be baptized.
- ❖ The church must discipline sinners and excommunicate them if necessary.
- ❖ Only those worthy of Communion should partake of it.
- ❖ Christians must be separate from the world in their habits.
- ❖ Christians must not fight evil persons or take part in the government.
- ❖ Ministers should be aided by the congregation and be promptly replaced if imprisoned, banished, or killed.
- ❖ Christians must not swear oaths.

First the Swiss Brethren copied the statement by hand; then they printed it. Soon it was hard to find one of the Brethren who did not have a copy of the Schleitheim Confession.

... A Sign in the Fire

This statement helped to draw the Swiss Brethren together. It helped to save some of them from becoming fanatics like other Anabaptists.

Michael Sattler's own congregation in southern Germany was in Catholic territory. Whereas Protestants drowned heretics, Catholics burned many of theirs. After Sattler returned to his home area and was arrested, he was not altogether surprised when he was sentenced to have his tongue cut out, to be tortured with red-hot tongs, and finally to be burned. Since Sattler would not be able to speak at his execution, he privately agreed with his brethren on another sign of faithfulness they would recognize. Sure enough, as he stood in the flames, once the ropes burned off his hands, he raised the index fingers of both hands as a sign of steadfastness to the end.

In a loving farewell letter to his people, Michael Sattler wrote that he would have wished to labor a little longer for the Lord on earth. However, he said, "The Lord is able to raise up another laborer to finish this work."

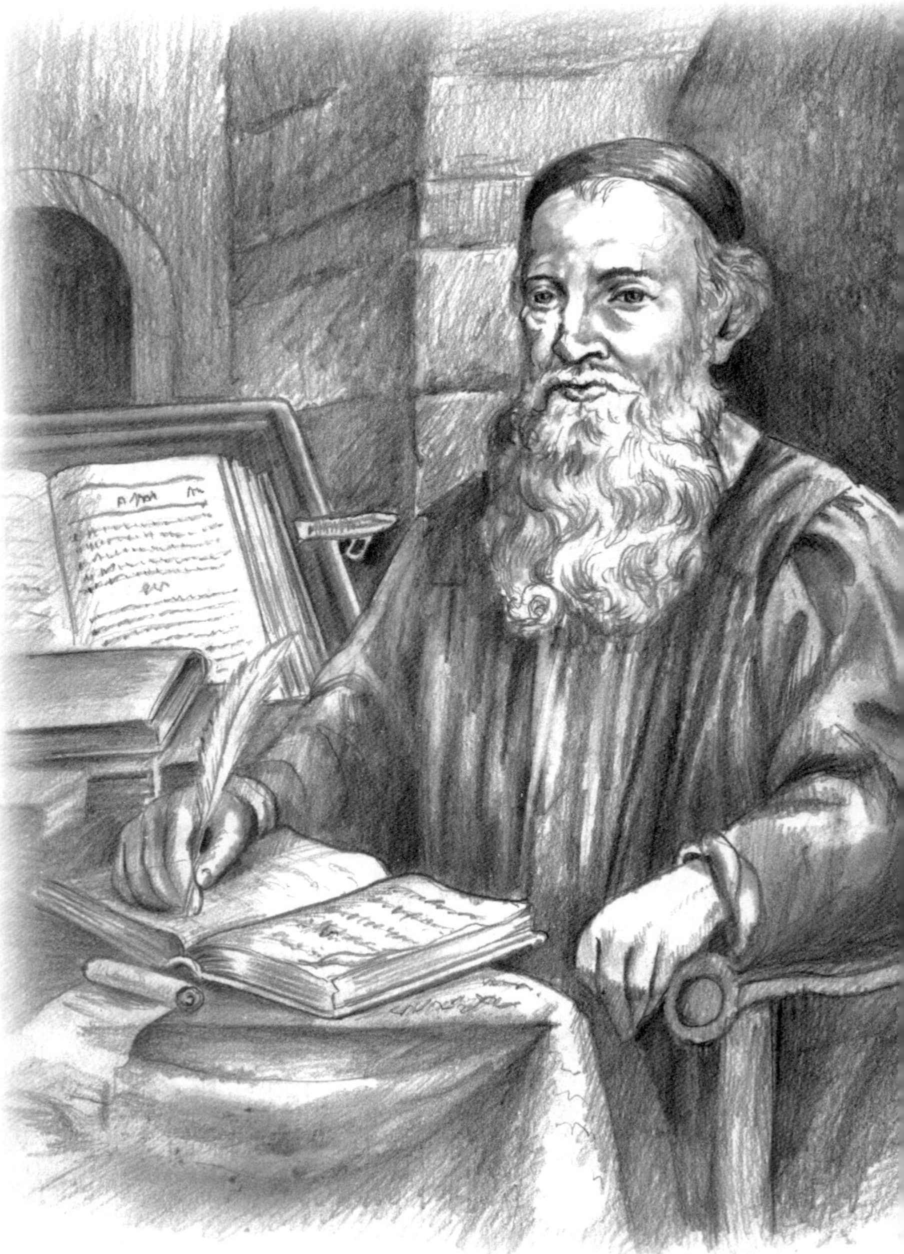

Menno Simons

A Good Name for the Anabaptists

(AD 1496–1559)

While Columbus was still taking his voyages to America, Menno Simons was born at Witmarsum, a village in the Netherlands. Although we know little of his boyhood, we know that he was well schooled. As an adult, he knew Latin quite well and had some knowledge of Greek.

Menno became a priest and settled down to have a comfortable life. He spent a fair amount of time with his buddies, drinking and playing cards.

But one day, he had a disturbing thought. What if the bread and wine of the Mass were not actually the body and blood of Christ, as the church had always taught? The idea haunted him, even though he confessed it to God and to another priest.

Menno Simons . . .

Where could he turn for help? Like other Catholics of that time, Menno believed it dangerous to study the Bible. He knew of people who had come to disagree with the church after they had read the Bible! But finally he decided that since the Bible is the Word of God, he would not be far wrong to study it.

In his own words, "At last I decided to read the New Testament once through diligently. I had not gone far with it before I became aware that we had been deceived."[8] No doubt Menno had found Jesus' words to His disciples, "Take, eat; this is my body" (Matthew 26:26). But as he examined the context, he saw that Jesus said these words the night before He was crucified. He used the bread and the cup only as symbols; they were not His actual flesh and blood.

Menno said little about what he had discovered. Although his preaching changed somewhat because he preached more directly from the Bible, he kept right on serving as priest. But then he heard news that unsettled him again. A man named Sicke Snyder had been burned at the stake in the Netherlands for being baptized the second time. To prove the man either right or wrong, Menno turned again to the Scriptures. Here again he found that his church and the Bible said two different things. Nowhere in the New Testament could he find a place where an infant had been baptized. Only believers were baptized.

About this time, other people were reading the Bible for themselves and discovering, like Menno, that the church was teaching errors. Some of them broke away from the church.

---

8   E. H. Broadbent, *The Pilgrim Church* (Port Colborne, ON: Gospel Folio Press, 2013), p. 201

...A Good Name for the Anabaptists

Regrettably, a number of these people made errors of their own. The most well-known group of such people seized the town of Münster in Germany. When an army besieged the city to recapture it, these people fought against the army. Finally starvation weakened them, their enemies recaptured the city, and the leaders of the heretics were tortured to death. Since these people baptized adults, they were called Anabaptists, and they gave the Anabaptists a very bad name.

Menno was not deceived by all this. He saw clearly that some people who disagreed with the Catholic Church were right and others were wrong. He saw that not only the people of Münster, but also many other teachers of Protestant doctrine were doing wrong. He himself was also in error because he continued to live an ungodly life.

Then Menno heard news of some religious people who had seized a monastery called the Old Cloister. They had not harmed the monks, but when attacked, they fought back. Finally they were defeated, and a number of them were killed. One of the dead was Menno's own brother.

This news went straight to Menno's heart. These people had done wrong, but at least they had followed their conscience. He, Menno, was not even doing that. If he had stood up for the right, he might have been able to help these dear people. Their blood seemed to fall hot on his hands.

At last he knelt in despair, asked God to have mercy on him, and committed his whole life and future to God. Now that Menno had repented, he could freely preach repentance, but

Menno Simons . . .

he could not long continue in the Catholic Church. On January 30, 1536, he told his people he was resigning the priesthood and leaving the church. He was baptized and joined a group of Anabaptists.

Now Menno was an outlaw who could not long continue living at Witmarsum. He traveled here and there, accepting people's hospitality wherever they gave it.

Menno's abilities came to the attention of the leaders of his new church. They asked him if he would accept ordination as a minister. Menno knew this would bring upon him very heavy responsibilities and even more danger. However, after much consideration and prayer, he accepted.

Menno was not a great orator, but he was a good church administrator. He traveled widely, encouraging his people. And just as he expected, the wrath of the government came down on him. Emperor Charles V issued an edict offering one hundred gold guilders for Menno's capture. Anyone who gave him food or shelter or owned one of his books would be punished with death. A few people actually did pay for their kindness to Menno with their lives. One man had his house confiscated because he sheltered Menno's wife and children when Menno's wife was sick.

Despite all this, Menno was never caught. Sometimes he put his life in danger by talking to Catholic priests themselves, urging them to change their minds and their lives. In his later years, he, along with other Anabaptists, found shelter in a province of Denmark where a noble was sympathetic to the

... A Good Name for the Anabaptists

Anabaptists. Although this kept him safe when he was at home, he still traveled to the Netherlands, to Germany, and to other parts of Europe, keeping in touch with his people.

Today no one knows just where Menno Simons is buried, but his work lives on. He was so effective a leader that his followers came to be known as Mennonites. Other denominations that baptize adults can trace their thinking back to Menno's influence.

Menno also wrote much, and his writings can be found today in a thick book called *The Complete Writings of Menno Simons*. At the beginning of every piece he wrote were these words: "For other foundation can no man lay than that is laid, which is Jesus Christ" (1 Corinthians 3:11).

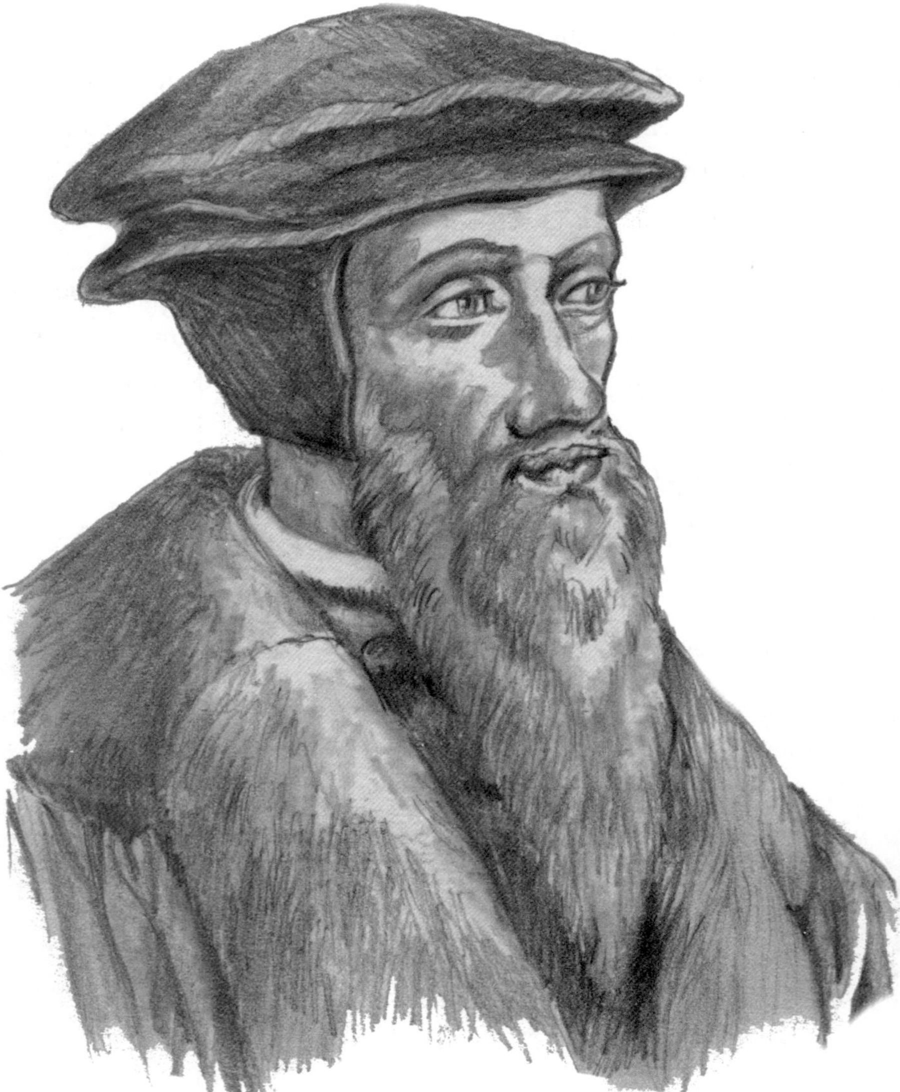

JOHN CALVIN

A TULIP TAKES FLOWER

(AD 1509–1564)

If ever there was a bookworm, it was John Calvin. Shy and quiet, but with a sharp mind, he read everything—the old literature, the writings of Augustine, and the Bible itself. In time, he became a very influential religious leader. What Luther was to Germany, and what Zwingli was to Switzerland, Calvin was to France.

As a young man, Calvin was stirred by the ideas of the Reformation and took them as his own principles. But since the French king was a committed Catholic, Calvin had to flee to Switzerland. There, at age twenty-six, he finished his first edition of *Institutes of the Christian Religion,* a book still in print today.

Always eager to learn more, Calvin decided to travel from Switzerland to Strasbourg, which today lies along the eastern border of France, but was then in western Germany. Hearing of warfare on the road ahead, he detoured through Geneva, Switzerland. He slipped into town with no idea but to find an inn, and so he was surprised when one of the church leaders of the city showed up to talk with him. The preacher, whose last name was Farel, urged him to stay in Geneva and help to improve conditions there. Calvin was not interested. He much preferred a life of reading and writing; he liked being quiet. He knew he would be in for stormy scenes if he tried to help govern the church at Geneva. So he said no. But Farel had a strong will too. Sternly he declared, "May God curse your studies if now in her time of need you refuse to lend your aid to His church!" Taken aback, Calvin agreed to stay.

Calvin was frail, and his health was poor. But he had a clear sense of purpose. He and Farel worked hard to put an end to the dancing, gambling, drinking, and immorality that went on in Geneva. Not surprisingly, the two men became very unpopular. In 1538 they were given three days to leave the city. Calvin and Farel went to Strasbourg, where Calvin had wanted to go in the first place. There he spent three of the happiest years of his life.

But back in Geneva, things were deteriorating. No one seemed to have a firm enough hand to stop people's loose living. So the city fathers called Calvin back. Once again, he did not want to live in Geneva. He feared more strife. At last he agreed to pay Geneva a visit, but made no other promises. However, the people were so eager to have him back that he finally agreed to stay.

As usual, Calvin drove himself, working early and late, eating little. His headaches and other physical ailments made him short-tempered. He was not impressed with Luther's failure to discipline his people, and he determined that nothing like that would happen at Geneva. Although Calvin made sure the government did not control the church, he made equally sure that the church controlled the government. He and his presbyters (counselors) established very strict laws. Everyone had to come to church. Not only did the council forbid card-playing, dancing, drunkenness, and gambling, it also gave some direction on the way people dressed and ate and what they named their babies.

Needless to say, Calvin became unpopular again with many people of Geneva. Once several men who had been excommunicated barged their way into church and demanded that Calvin serve Communion to them. But Calvin held his frail hands over the emblems, and they backed down. Recognizing Calvin as a man with a strong sense of mission, enough people supported him that he managed to keep control of the city. Outwardly, Geneva was quiet and orderly, and visitors were much impressed. Privately, however, the city council struggled with issues such as immorality among the citizens.

Penalties were severe. Geneva punished heretics with death. In fact, between 1542 and Calvin's own death in 1564, fifty-eight persons were executed. How could Calvin justify putting heretics to death? As many other people believed in his day, he argued that heretics are even worse than murderers. A murderer merely kills the body, but a heretic who deceives people destroys their souls.

John Calvin...

The best known of those executed was Michael Servetus, a doctor who helped to explain the circulation of the blood. For centuries, people had believed that blood traveled from one side of the heart to the other by somehow seeping through the septum, the wall dividing the heart in two. But around 1550, Servetus wrote that the passage of blood "does not take place through the septum—as commonly believed—but by another admirable contrivance, the blood being transmitted through the lungs, in the course of which it is elaborated and becomes of a crimson color."[9] He was exactly right, although it was a novel idea in those days. But what really got Servetus into trouble was his scoffing at doctrines that Calvin held dear. Servetus was in fact heretical on a number of points. The Geneva council imprisoned him and finally had him burned at the stake. Through the flames, Servetus cried, "O Jesus, thou Son of the eternal God, have pity on me."

What doctrinal beliefs drove John Calvin? Basically, he got them from Augustine. He said in effect, "This is where Augustine's doctrines take shape." Calvin's teachings may be summarized with the acronym TULIP.

> *Total depravity*—man is so totally fallen that he cannot do a thing to help himself spiritually.
>
> *Unconditional election*—God chooses (elects) who will be saved. Calvin taught double predestination: God also chooses who will be lost.

---

[9] Raymond F. Jones, *Stories of Great Physicians* (Racine, WI: Whitman Publishing, 1963), p. 82.

Limited atonement—Christ died only for those whom God had already chosen to be saved.

Irresistible grace—If God chooses to save a person, that person cannot resist God's choice.

Perseverance of saints—all those chosen by God will be faithful to the end.

Many Calvinists today do not claim to believe all these points. They believe at least in the perseverance of saints, popularly called "once saved, always saved." But the more you study these points, the more it is clear that they all depend on each other. If you believe one, you must believe them all, for they are based on the idea that God makes all the choices and man makes none.

Calvin admitted that he himself could not fully explain his doctrines. He did not altogether know why "God has once for all determined both whom He would admit to salvation, and whom He would condemn to destruction." But he urged his readers to submit to "a just and irreprehensible, but incomprehensible, judgment."[10]

Martin Luther struggled with the same problem. He admitted, "Such a concept of God seems wicked, cruel, and intolerable, and by it many men have been revolted in all ages. . . . Natural reason, however much it is offended, must admit the consequences of the omniscience and omnipotence of God."[11]

---

[10] *Institutes*, II, xxi, 7, cited in Durant, p. 464.
[11] Roland Bainton, *Here I Stand: on the Life of Martin Luther*, pp. 254–255, cited in Durant, p. 435.

John Calvin... A TULIP Takes Flower

Is there a better balance to be found? Certainly God is sovereign over all human affairs. But if we admit that God wants humans to make a few choices of their own and not just be puppets, it is easier to explain many Scriptures that Calvin dismissed. Someone offering to strike a good balance put it this way: "Pray as if it all depended on God; work as if it all depended on you." That may be oversimplified, but it is not a bad rule of thumb.

John Calvin was a very influential man, in some ways more influential than Luther. Calvin wrote letters to church leaders all over Europe, and they wrote to him. His *Institutes of the Christian Religion* went through several revisions, and the final one was five times as big as the first one. It has over a thousand pages and fills four volumes. The first one speaks of God the Father; the second speaks of Christ's work; the third deals with the Holy Spirit; and the fourth speaks of the church and how it relates to the civil government.

In France, Calvin's followers were called Huguenots. In the Netherlands, they were called members of the Reformed church, as they are today. The Pilgrims and Puritans were Calvinists. So was John Knox, who brought Calvinism to Scotland.

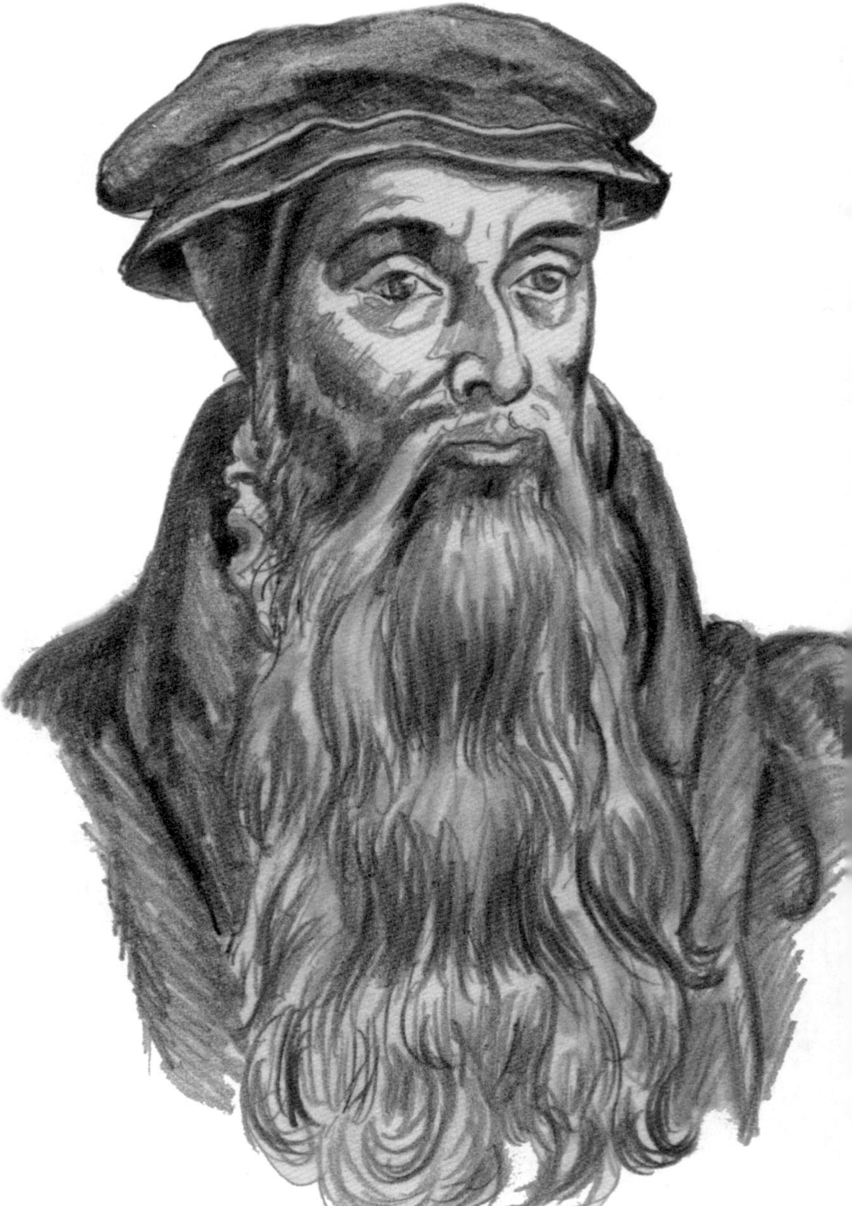

John Knox

The Reformation Comes to Scotland

(AD 1515?–1572)

When John Knox was born in poor, out-of-the-way Scotland, nobody important paid attention. As a man, he became one of history's noted preachers and church leaders.

John Knox was born in the 1500s, which, as we know, came just after Columbus's first trip to America. Exciting things were happening in Europe, not only because explorers were taking new journeys to new places, but also because religious leaders were rising with new ideas. They had to be brave, for their new ideas put them in danger of being martyred.

John Knox started out as a loyal Catholic and became a priest. Then he began to listen to Protestant ideas. He even joined a group of Protestants who had seized a castle along the seacoast in hope that Protestant England would send them support. Sadly

John Knox . . .

for them, the queen then ruling Scotland, Mary of Guise, sent for help to the Catholic French! A French fleet showed up and took the rebels captive, including John Knox.

Soon he found out what it was like to be a French galley slave. For hours a day, he had to pull an oar in unison with other slaves. How could he do it without wearing out? Once he felt the whiplash of the slave driver, he knew how. He had to. Hour after hour, week after week, month after month, the agony went on.

After nineteen months, the English government finally worked out a release for John and his comrades. John could finally straighten his aching back and decide where to go next. Back to Scotland? No, the Catholics were still too strong there. So John preached in England.

However, after a few years, John heard bad news. England had a new queen. Her name was also Mary—Mary Tudor, to be exact. Like Mary of Guise, she was a Catholic. Mary persecuted Protestants, who began to call her "Bloody Mary." John fled to mainland Europe and eventually made his way to Geneva in Switzerland, where he met John Calvin. He was much impressed with Calvin's ideas and made them his own.

While John Knox was in Geneva, Protestants kept stirring the pot back in Scotland, and John returned to join the growing movement. A new Queen of Scots had taken the throne there—still another Mary! This was the daughter of Mary of Guise. Like her mother, she was a Catholic. Mary was beautiful and intelligent, and had she been wise, she might have won Scotland for the Catholic Church. But she married foolishly

... The Reformation Comes to Scotland

once and again, and she got involved in plots she should have stayed out of. The people of Scotland learned to mistrust her, and her power weakened. In 1560, the Scottish Parliament declared Protestantism to be the religion of Scotland whether Mary liked it or not.

The Protestants established a Presbyterian form of government. What others might call church district meetings, they would call *presbyteries.* Larger groups of church leaders were called *synods,* and countrywide meetings were called *general assemblies.* Churches with a Presbyterian form of government may also be called Reformed, as the Dutch Reformed church is in the Netherlands.

Like Calvin, Knox controlled the church and kept a sharp eye on the government. His preaching was fiery; people sometimes thought he would shake the pulpit apart. When he died in 1572, he had established a strong Presbyterian church. "Give me Scotland, or I die!" he had cried, and he got his Scotland.

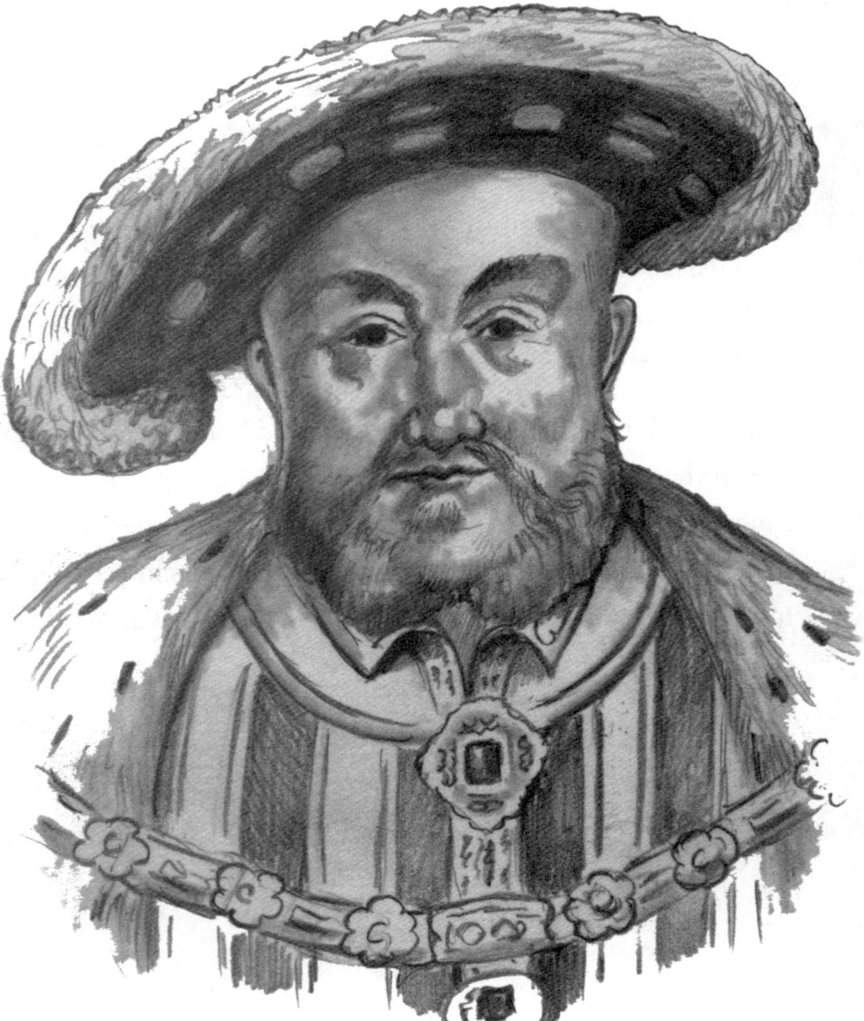

Henry VIII

The Reformation Begins in England

(AD 1491–1547)

Henry VIII was hardly the man you would expect to begin a religious reformation. He did not expect to himself. As a young king, he was a loyal Catholic. In fact, he wrote a book against heretics, called the *Seven Sacraments*. The pope was so pleased with the book that he gave Henry the title "Defender of the Faith," and English kings and queens have kept that title to this day.

But Henry VIII lived during changing times. Luther, Tyndale, Calvin, Knox, and Menno Simons all lived during his lifetime. The hold of the Roman Catholic Church was loosening, even in England. To many English people, the pope seemed like a faraway prince who wanted too much of their money.

Henry VIII ...

The seeds of trouble began when Henry's shrewd father, King Henry VII, decided that a marriage between his family and the royal family in Spain would keep England and Spain friendly with each other. He had his son Arthur (Henry's older brother) marry Catherine, the daughter of the famous Ferdinand and Isabella. But Arthur died five months later.

Not to be outdone, the king decided Catherine should marry Henry, his next son in line for the throne. However, the Catholic Church had a rule that a man must never marry his brother's widow. To get past this, the royal family got the pope to make a special exception for Henry and Catherine. They were married about the time that Henry became king.

Henry and Catherine lived together for eighteen years and had five children. But here again, death intervened, for only one child lived, a girl named Mary. Henry very much wanted to have a son to be the next king. He began to wonder if his marriage to Catherine was proper after all. To add to his doubts, another woman had caught his eye—Catherine's maid of honor, whose name was Ann Boleyn.

Henry appealed to the pope for a divorce. But the appeal had to go through England's powerful Cardinal Wolsey, and Wolsey moved slowly. Being a forceful king, Henry stripped Cardinal Wolsey of his offices and property, and later bade him come to London to answer for treason. Wolsey, fallen and crushed, said, "If I had served God as diligently as I have done the king, He would not have in my age given me over to my enemies." He set out for London but died on the way.

. . . The Reformation Begins in England

As to the pope, he had other people to please besides Henry—for instance, Catherine's nephew Charles V. Charles was emperor of the Holy Roman Empire and could cause the pope more trouble than Henry ever could.

At last Henry decided to take things into his own hands. He had Parliament declare that the pope had no authority over the churches in England. The following year, 1534, he enacted another law called the Act of Supremacy, which declared that the king "justly and rightfully is and ought to be the supreme head of the Church of England." Enough English people agreed to, or at least did not object to, this move that Henry could get away with it.

At that point, Henry still considered himself a Catholic. But now that he had turned his country loose from the pope's direction, the churches in England began to make changes. Perhaps most important was that Henry's agents closed the monasteries, first the small ones and then the larger ones, and confiscated their property.

Did Henry get his Anne? Oh, yes, and she bore him a bouncing baby... daughter! They named her Elizabeth, but Henry was desperate for a son. Later he found Anne guilty of unfaithfulness to him, had her beheaded, and married again. The third wife, Jane Seymour, finally had a boy named Edward. Henry had three more wives after Jane.

After Henry died in 1547, the kingdom went to nine-year-old Edward. Edward VI was sickly and died of tuberculosis before his sixteenth birthday. Nevertheless, England continued

Henry VIII... The Reformation Begins in England

to move away from the Catholic Church. For instance, images were removed from the churches.

The next in line for the throne, since Henry had no other living sons, was Henry and Catherine's oldest daughter Mary. Mary was Catholic like her grandparents, and she tried to bring England back under Catholic authority. Mary was not a cruel person by nature. But she believed, as many did in those days, that anyone who taught against the Catholic Church was a heretic and deserved death. Nearly three hundred people were put to death during her reign, and the English people began to call her "Bloody Mary."

But Mary did not have enough time. She reigned for only a little over five years, and when she died in 1558, all her efforts were lost. Her half-sister Elizabeth, who was minded like her father, ruled for many years. Although struggles continued, the Protestants had the upper hand from then on. The Church of England today is also called the Anglican Church. The Episcopalian Church in the United States has its roots in the Anglican Church.

Did Henry VIII at least have a grandson to carry on his name? That is an interesting question. Like Edward, Mary was not well and had no children. Elizabeth never married. When Elizabeth died, her cousin James I took the throne. So it turned out that Henry VIII, who was so eager to keep up the royal family line, had no royal grandchildren at all.

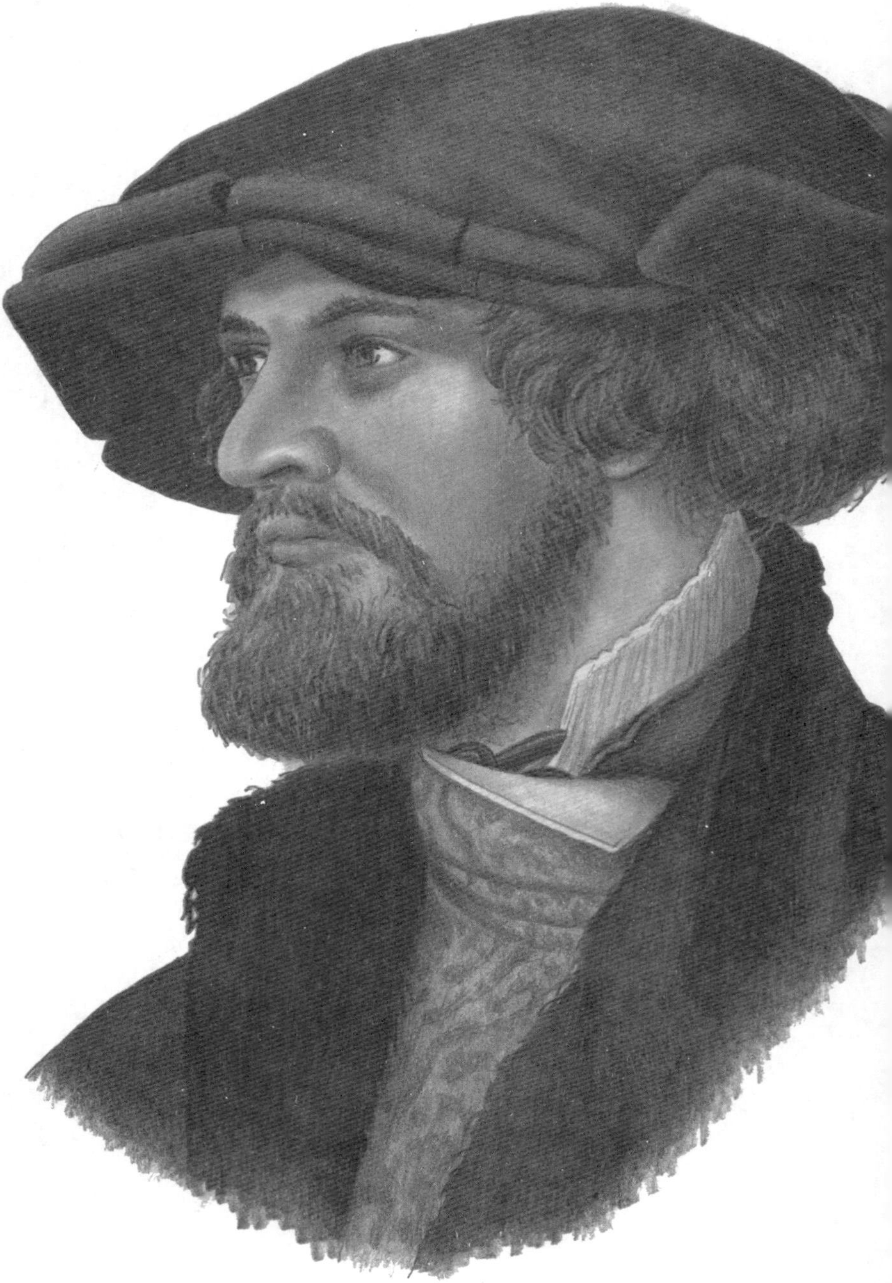

WILLIAM TYNDALE

A New Bible for English Readers

(AD 1492?–1536)

We would be better off without God's law than without the pope's!" So said a respected church leader to William Tyndale. In those days, when Henry VIII was first king, England was still Catholic. Many church leaders were very ignorant of the Scriptures. They could not quote the Lord's Prayer and did not even care that they couldn't. All they cared about was what the pope said. But Tyndale declared, "I defy the pope and all his laws! If God spare my life, ere many years I will cause a boy that driveth the plow to know more of the Scriptures than thou dost."

Tyndale's firm stand made him very unpopular, and he had to leave the cozy home where he had been staying with friends. After living here and there, he decided there was no safe place for him in England. He had a secret project—and a dangerous one—to translate the Bible into English. The king and the church leaders did not approve of translating the Bible into English.

William Tyndale...

They thought Latin was good enough. If ordinary people could not read it, so much the better! Giving them the Bible in their own language might make them disagree with the church.

In 1524, William Tyndale sailed for Hamburg, Germany. Translating the New Testament took him only a year. But who would print it for him? No one in Hamburg seemed to have a printing press, so Tyndale went to Cologne.

The printers in Cologne got busy with the project. But soon an important Catholic named John Cochlaeus heard a rumor that men in Cologne were working against the church. He befriended the printers' workmen over glasses of wine, asked them questions, and learned what Tyndale was doing. Quickly Cochlaeus warned the king of England to beware of ships coming across the English Channel with Bibles smuggled in bales of cloth and barrels of other goods. He notified other church authorities too, and sent agents to arrest William Tyndale.

But in the meantime, a remorseful workman had confessed to Tyndale. By the time Cochlaeus's agents arrived, Tyndale and an assistant had scooped up his papers and the already-printed pages and slipped away, this time to Worms. There the printing was finished.

Officials tried to stop the smuggling of English Testaments, but Tyndale's Testaments came later than they expected, after they had stopped inspecting the shipping. Suddenly they realized that thousands of the Testaments were already in England. They searched houses, seizing Testaments and arresting people who had them. At last they had 158 baskets of Tyndale's

Testaments. They took them to a public place called Paul's Cross and burned them.

The authorities also tried to stop Tyndale's work from ever leaving the shores of mainland Europe. The bishop of London tried buying Tyndale's New Testaments brand-new to keep them out of people's hands. He contacted a merchant named Packington, whom he thought could help him. A historian named Halle tells us the story.

[Packington] said to the bishop, "My lord, if it be your pleasure, I can in this matter do more, I dare say, than most of the merchants of England that are here . . . so that if it be your lordship's pleasure to pay for them . . . I will then assure you to have every book of them that is imprinted and is here unsold."

"Gentle Mr. Packington, do your diligence and get them; and with all my heart I will pay for them whatsoever they cost you, for the books are erroneous and naught, and I intend surely to destroy them all, and to burn them at Paul's Cross."

But then Mr. Packington privately went to William Tyndale. "William," he said, "I know that thou art a poor man and hast a heap of New Testaments and books by thee, for the which thou hast both endangered thy friends and beggared thyself; and I have now gotten thee a merchant."

"Who is the merchant?"

"The bishop of London."

"Oh," said Tyndale, "that is because he will burn them." Then he caught the gleam in Packington's eye and said, "I am the gladder, for these two benefits shall come thereof: I shall get money to bring myself out of debt, and the whole world will cry out against the burning of God's Word." The money he received helped to support him while he improved his translation and printed a new edition.

Halle added that after this, the revised Testament "came thick and three-fold over into England."[12]

But Worms was becoming less and less safe for Tyndale. He moved from place to place in Germany, and then to Antwerp, in what is now Belgium. There he could work on translating the Old Testament while he kept in touch with travelers from England. He spent a good part of his time befriending and helping persecuted English refugees and other unfortunate people. One of the friends he made was a young man named Henry Phillips. One day as they left the house together, two men standing in the street seized and arrested Tyndale. Only then did Tyndale realize that Phillips was a traitor.

Tradition says that although he was in prison, Tyndale kept on translating the Bible. He had befriended the keeper's family, and under his influence, they had become converted. "If he be not a good Christian man," they said, "we know not whom to trust." Gladly they gave him candles, paper, a Hebrew Bible, a dictionary, and whatever else he might need. By the time he died, Tyndale had translated the Old Testament through Chronicles.

---

12 Violet Wood, *Great Is the Company* (NY: Friendship Press, 1955).

. . . A New Bible for English Readers

At last, on October 6, 1536, William Tyndale was taken from prison, publicly strangled, and burned. His last recorded words were a prayer: "Lord, open the King of England's eyes."

God was already answering Tyndale's prayer. A bishop in England named Miles Coverdale had made an English translation of the Bible—approved by the English authorities—using much of Tyndale's work! And in later years, Bible translators used Tyndale's work again. In fact, when you read the King James Version, you often read Tyndale's forceful, graceful choice of words.

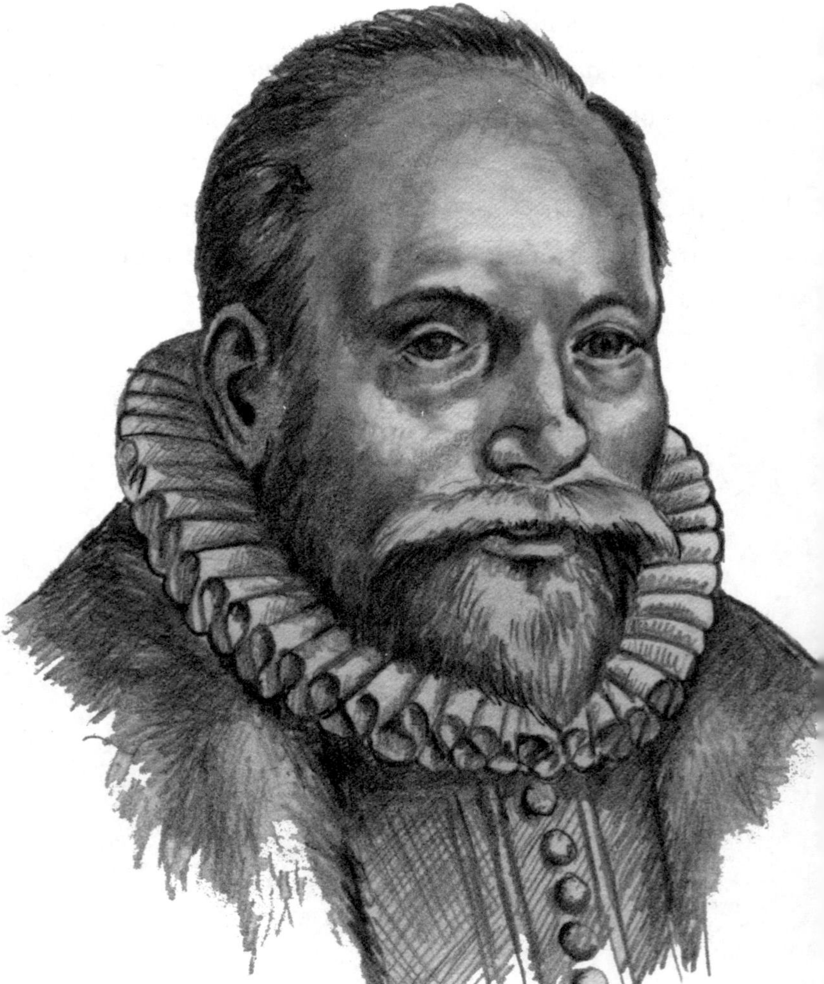

Jacobus Arminius

A Calvinist Who Changed His Mind

(AD 1560–1609)

Jacobus Arminius was Dutch like Menno Simons, and he was born the year after Menno died. At that time, Philip II of Spain ruled the Netherlands. Being Catholic, he persecuted the Dutch Calvinists. While Jacobus was quite young, Spanish marauders destroyed his town, and Jacobus was left with no parents or close relatives. Kind friends took him in and sent him to school. Jacobus proved so bright that he went on to study at Leyden as well as in Switzerland and Italy.

Returning to the Netherlands, Jacobus was ordained in 1588, the year of Philip's ill-fated Spanish Armada. Later he became professor of theology at the University of Leyden.

Jacobus Arminius...

People thought he was an ideal preacher—his preaching was clear, and his personal example was good.

But trouble was brewing. Some people in the Netherlands were arguing that there should be freedom of worship for all. This grew naturally out of the idea that God gives everyone the freedom to make his own choices. But the Reformed Church members, who were Calvinists, wanted freedom only for their own faith. All others, they thought, should be forced into their church. The Reformed leaders looked to Arminius for help. Since he was a clear thinker, speaker, and writer, would he please prove from the Bible that the people who wanted these freedoms were wrong?

Arminius took up the challenge. He studied the new teachings and compared them to the Bible. But then an unexpected problem took place. He began to agree with the new teachings! He became troubled with the Calvinist idea that God makes all the choices for mankind. This then must mean that people are puppets and that the many sinners in the world are lost because God chose it for them. The God of the Bible, the God he knew, did not fit this description.

Arminius's beliefs crept into his teachings, and the young pastors he was teaching began echoing his teachings in their own churches. His fellow churchmen became alarmed. When they asked Arminius about these rumors, it was just as they feared. He would not say he was against Calvinism, but neither did he say he believed all that Calvinists were teaching.

Deeply troubled by the uproar that surrounded him, Arminius died before he was fifty. But his followers kept his doctrine

... A Calvinist Who Changed His Mind

alive. They urged the church to do what Arminius had recommended—convene a general church council to consider the matter. They believed basically that (1) man has no power over evil in himself, but he has the God-given power to choose for God or against Him; (2) God chooses people who choose Him, (3) Christ died for all, giving everyone an opportunity to choose salvation, (4) humans can resist God's grace, and (5) God keeps His people, but a Christian finally gets to heaven only if he keeps up his relationship with the Lord.

It was a slow-moving age, and not until nine years after Arminius died did the church council gather. In the meantime, in writings and sermons, the two disagreeing sides kept up a lively argument. In fact, unfortunately, the disagreement nearly brought Holland to civil war.[13]

At last the council, also known as a synod, met in Dort (Dortrecht). Reformed church leaders came from Switzerland, Germany, England, and other parts of Holland. The synod lasted from November 13, 1618, to May 9, 1619. The result: Arminius's ideas were unanimously condemned! Arminians were forbidden to hold public services. Many of them fled to England.

But the ideas Arminius had promoted continued to live on. John Wesley taught them in England, and the teachings spread to America. Today many people who know they are not Calvinists, do not realize that they follow the teachings of Jacobus Arminius. "Jacob who?"

---

13 Durant, p. 460.

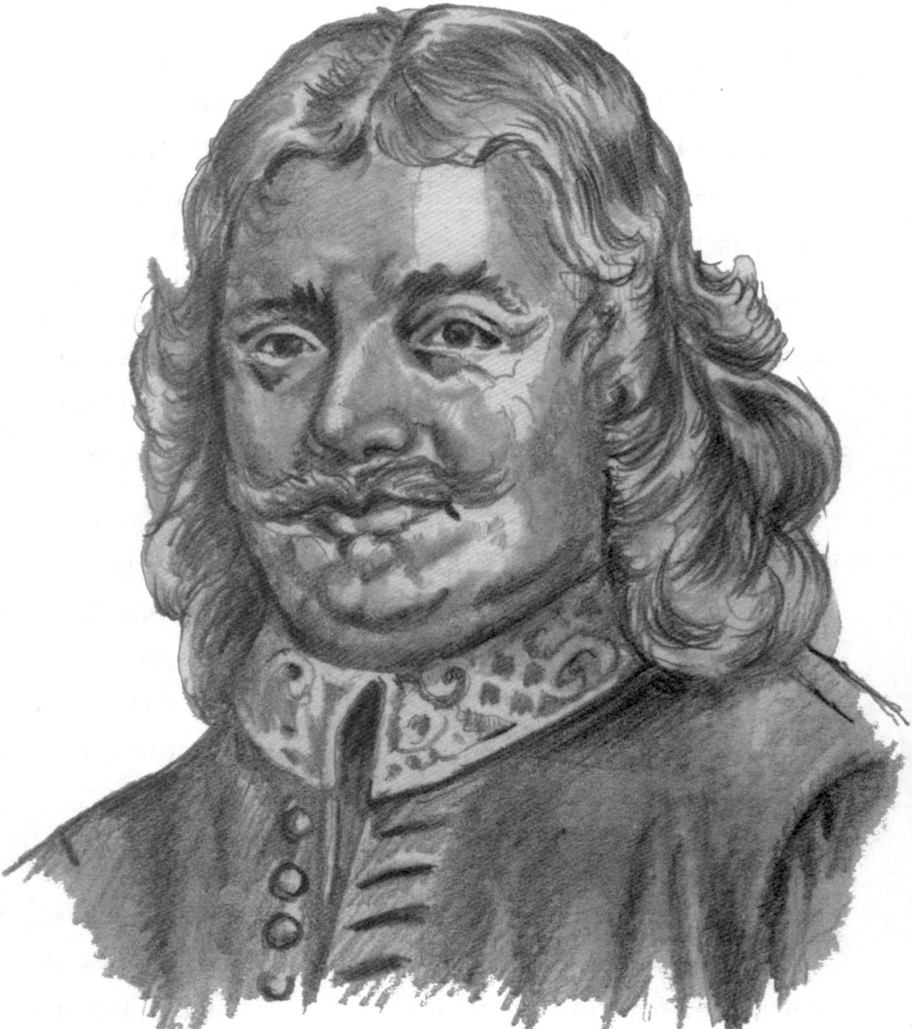

John Bunyan

A Pilgrim Who Progressed

(AD 1628–1688)

News traveled slowly in 1649, but this news must have traveled faster than most. Charles I, king of England, had been beheaded. John Bunyan turned twenty-one that year. He had fought against King Charles under the stern general Oliver Cromwell. Now Cromwell took control of the government and came to be called the Lord Protector of England.

Although John's struggle in the army was over, he still had struggles within. He knew he was living an ungodly life. One day he was cursing and swearing in his usual way until a neighbor woman who was not a godly person herself told him she trembled to hear him. Her rebuke sobered him, and he tried hard to clean up his language. He read the Bible and tried to keep the Ten Commandments. But something was missing.

John Bunyan...

When he married, his wife brought him her tiny library of two books—*The Plain Man's Pathway to Heaven* and *The Practice of Piety*. At first John thought it was not his kind of reading. "A ballad or a news-book," he said afterward, "would have pleased me better." However, he read to his wife from her books. When his oldest daughter, Mary, was born blind, he believed that God was punishing him.

John was a tinker, a mender of pots and pans. To earn a living, he traveled around, visiting villages near his home. One day he ran across several women sitting in a sunny doorway discussing Scripture. John slipped closer to hear what they had to say. He soon discovered that these ladies knew something more than the Bible; they knew the Lord Himself. They had a restful, trustful relationship with the Lord that John did not have.

The testimony of these ladies gripped him. Although he felt bad to realize how far away from the truth he had been, at least now he had some new steppingstones. More passages of the Bible started to make sense to him. Finally John found salvation through trusting what Jesus Christ did for him on Calvary.

After he was converted, he had a new peace, but he had new struggles too. One early morning before he got out of bed, the odd thought came to him, "Why not sell Jesus, the way Judas did?" "Of course not," he thought. "Not for anything." But the thought persisted until suddenly he thought, "All right, sell Him!" Then he realized what he had done. He felt like a bird shot out of a tree. How could he ever be right with God again?

. . . A Pilgrim Who Progressed

Bunyan wrote later of his struggles in a book called *Grace Abounding to the Chief of Sinners.* Sometimes he thought he would see a little hope; then down he would go again. Once he told his experience to a Christian brother and said he feared he had sinned beyond forgiveness—and the brother said he thought so too! Bunyan wrote later that he had gotten "cold comfort" that time. Still, he decided that if he were to die, he would die at the foot of the cross. This was perhaps the wisest decision he ever made.

At last he found peace in the thought, "Thy righteousness is in heaven." He was able to help others find their way with the Lord, and he became a preacher.

As long as Cromwell ruled, Bunyan had the liberty to preach. But when Cromwell died in 1658, the picture changed. In 1660, Charles II, son of the beheaded monarch, came to the throne. Once again, the Church of England took control. Although Charles II was not eager to persecute people of various faiths, Parliament had other ideas. Parliament declared that the Church of England's *Book of Common Prayer* must be used in all services.

Of course, not everyone agreed to this. Like other dissenting preachers, John Bunyan preached illegally. Arrested and tried in court, he was sentenced to prison. The judge told him if he kept on preaching illegally, he would be hanged. Bunyan replied, "If they would let me out of prison today, I should, God helping me, be preaching the Gospel again tomorrow."

John Bunyan...

It is one thing to be brave in court; it is another thing to be brave day after endless day in a depressing prison cell. John felt that "parting with my wife and poor children" was "like pulling the flesh from my bones." How would the family survive? And how could he serve his congregation?

At least the family could visit him there in the Bedford Jail, and he could make laces for them to sell. And he could serve as pastor to the other men in prison. Quite a few of them were dissenters too. John also did some writing to help pay the bills.

Months passed, but no word came for Bunyan's release. The jailor himself grew impatient with the government's slowness to release John. He let Bunyan slip out sometimes to visit his people.

John stayed in prison year after year for six years. At last he was allowed to go home. True to his word, John promptly began preaching again. The king's agents interrupted the meeting and stuck him back into jail!

Would this time in jail be as long as last time? Indeed! He spent another six years there. At last the king passed a law that set the dissenters free. But three years later, Parliament passed another law reversing the king's law, and John went back to jail. Once again, he had pen and paper, which his family brought when they visited him. Once again, he settled down to do some writing. John did not know how long he would spend in jail, so he made the time count. This time he was released after six months.

Later he told the story of how he came to write the *Pilgrim's Progress*. He wanted to write some other book, but illustrations kept coming to his mind that did not fit the book. So he thought he would set them down on a separate paper to get them out of his mind. The trouble was, he kept getting more inspirations until the separate paper ended up being a stack of papers—a book of its own!

The *Pilgrim's Progress* was an allegory, like a parable. It told the story of how a man with a huge burden on his back set out walking from the City of Destruction toward the Celestial City. The difficult hills, gloomy hollows, dangerous giants, treacherous enemies, and faithful friends he met along the way all stood for things John had experienced or had seen other people going through.

At first some of John's friends thought the book too much like a fairy tale, but he had it printed anyhow. And readers loved it! It turned out to be John Bunyan's best-loved book.

Prison life was now in the past. For another twelve years or so, John could spend more time at home with his family and minister to his people. But his time was running out. One day he set out on horseback for a forty-mile trip to settle a family disagreement. On the way back, he got caught in heavy rain. He became ill with pneumonia and died a few days later.

Nevertheless, the words of John Bunyan's books echo today. People have read millions of copies of *Pilgrim's Progress* in hundreds of languages. Where the Bible has traveled, the *Pilgrim's Progress* has gone too, "as the singing bird follows the dawn."

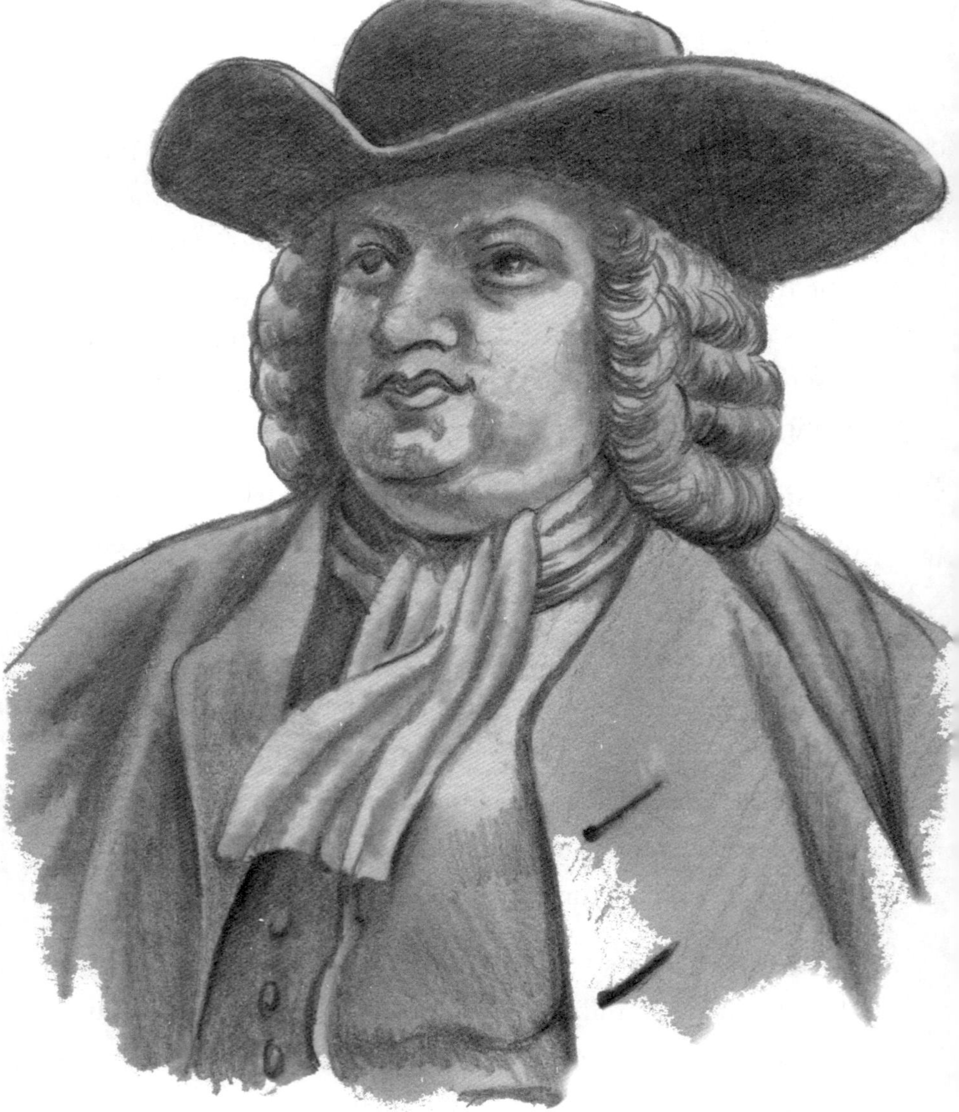

WILLIAM PENN

THE MAN PENNSYLVANIA WAS NOT NAMED AFTER

(AD 1644–1718)

William Penn was the most famous Quaker who ever lived, but he was not the first Quaker by any means. The Quaker movement began when William was about three years old. He himself grew up in the Church of England. He was the son of Admiral William Penn, and an early painting of young William pictures him in armor.

In college, William went to a secret meeting where George Fox, the founder of the Quakers, preached. (Fox had once told a judge to "tremble at the Word of the Lord," and the judge scoffingly called him a "quaker." Quakers themselves called each other Friends.) Fox's sermon opened a new world

William Penn ...

of thought to William, and William resolved to lay aside his worldly dress and ideas.

William's father was distressed and angry. To get these new notions out of William's head, he sent him to France and Italy. The strategy seemed to work, for William slipped into fashionable ways again. Then his father sent him to manage the family estate in Ireland. But there William met another Quaker who revived the old flame in his heart, and he became a Quaker for life. William was twenty-two years old.

At that time, Quakers were persecuted in England. William was laying aside a life of power and luxury for much trouble. He did in fact go to prison three times. Nevertheless he wrote a book while in prison called *No Cross, No Crown,* defending his Quaker beliefs.

When William's father died, his possessions came into William's hands. King Charles II had owed a large debt to Admiral Penn. Now he owed it to William. William suggested to the king that instead of paying him the sixteen thousand pounds he owed, he grant William a section of land in North America. This solved the king's problem and gave William Penn and his Quaker friends a fresh start in a faraway land.

William told the king he hoped to call his land Sylvania (wooded region). The king said, "We will call the land *Penn-sylvania.*" William said, "It is against Quaker principles to name a place after oneself." The king replied, "We are not naming it after you; we are naming it after your father." So every time we

... THE MAN PENNSYLVANIA WAS NOT NAMED AFTER

say "Pennsylvania," we hark back to a decision made by the English government.

William did not come to Pennsylvania immediately, but in 1682 he crossed the Atlantic in a ship called the *Welcome* and sailed up the Delaware to the town he had named Philadelphia. (*Phil* means "brotherly love," and *adelphia* means "city.") William had his own ideas about how to govern the land. Quakers did not believe in war. He knew that other colonies fought the Indians, but he was determined to keep peace with them. For one thing, he did not think the land was his just because the king had given it to him. He bought it also from the Indians. He called his way of governing the "Holy Experiment."

William Penn advertised heavily in Europe, inviting people to come to Pennsylvania. He did not persecute people of any other faith. Thousands of Quakers came to Pennsylvania, and many others of various religions came too.

However, not everyone who came to Pennsylvania agreed with William's way of governing. The Scotch-Irish pioneers who moved out to the perimeters of the colony believed they had to fight the Indians. In 1756, after a disagreement that lasted for years after William died, most of the Quakers gave up their seats in the governing Assembly, and men governed Pennsylvania who believed in paying bullet for bullet.

William faced challenges it is hard for us to understand today. The land had not been well surveyed. Mapmakers made guesses that turned out to be very wrong. William had a serious

WILLIAM PENN ...

disagreement with Lord Baltimore of Maryland over where the line between Pennsylvania and Maryland should be placed. It was long after both of them had died that two surveyors drew a line between the two colonies that came to be called the Mason-Dixon Line.

In his later life, William faced some unhappy developments. He had grown up living in mansions, having servants, and eating the best of food. Despite becoming a Quaker, he never learned to lay that lifestyle aside. His habits cost him quite a bit of money. At the same time, he traveled here and there at his own expense, trying to win support for Quakers. He wrote and published various books and pamphlets, also at his own expense.

The king's huge grant of Pennsylvania did not enrich William. By the time he was finished paying all the costs of advertising, going through paperwork, paying administrators, buying the land from the Indians, and selling the land cheap or giving some of it away, he actually lost. Many people did not pay their bills to William. Most frustrating of all, he kept owing more and more to his manager back in England—at least his manager said he did. After his manager died, the manager's family sued William for a figure he thought was unreasonable, and he ended up spending a year in debtor's prison. Prison life was bad for his health. A few years later, he suffered a stroke that left him paralyzed for the last six years of his life.

Although the closing years of his life were dark, most people prefer to remember him for his kindly, fair ways, his peaceable

... The Man Pennsylvania Was Not Named After

policies, and his ideas that served as good examples for others. Though he was human and made mistakes, William Penn earned an important place in history.

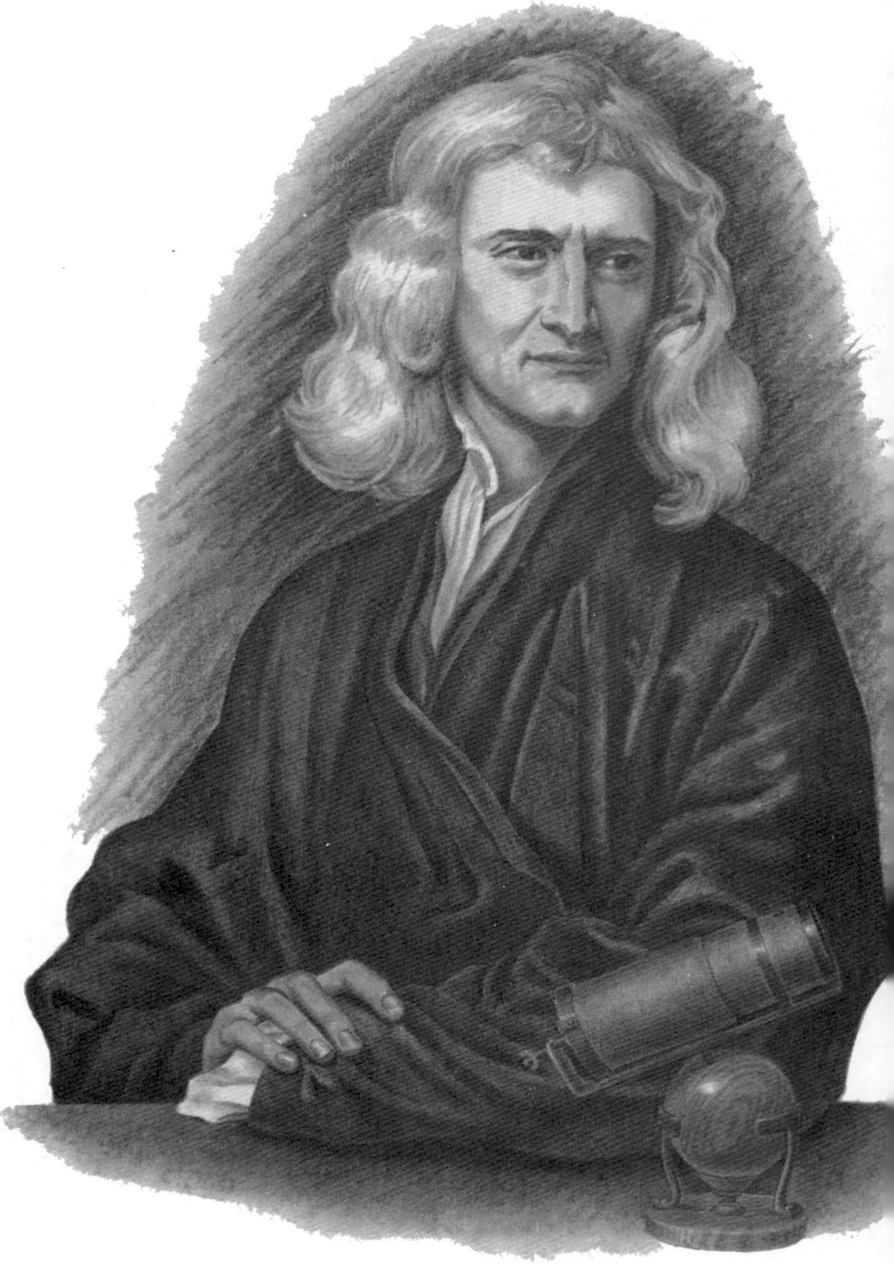

Isaac Newton

A Dreamer Who Made Good

(AD 1642–1727)

He was born on a cold Christmas Day in England. His young mother was already a widow. People said he was small enough to fit into a quart jar, and they feared he would not live.

But Isaac Newton not only lived; he turned out to be an unusual boy. What a way of thinking he had! He made a small working windmill, and then modified it so that a running mouse could power it to grind grain into flour. When a severe storm came up, he stayed out in the whipping wind, curious about it.

Isaac did poorly in school at first. Dreaminess kept interfering with his studies. Later he did much better. But when he was thirteen his stepfather died, and his mother called him home to tend the farm. Isaac meant to do well, but tending animals and cultivating rows of crops had little meaning for him. Once, it is said, he came home lost in thought, dragging an empty bridle, not realizing that the horse he had been leading had slipped out of it. His mother sent him back to school.

After Isaac finished school, he went on to Cambridge University. Here he did not shine as much as we might have expected, but perhaps we should not be surprised at this. He was kept so busy earning his room and board by doing odd jobs and serving professors their meals that he did not have as much time for study as he would have liked.

In 1665, the same year Isaac graduated, the dreaded bubonic plague swept through London. Chills, fever, and headache—when anyone felt these symptoms, he knew he was in trouble, especially if black spots formed under the skin. Thousands of people who came down with the disease died within a day or two. The university closed for a time, and Isaac went home. This time no one insisted that he spend his days farming, so Isaac had time to think.

One of the questions that scientists had often mulled over was "Why does the moon circle the earth? Everything else that moves travels in a straight line until something pulls it off course. What then keeps the moon curving around the earth instead of sailing straight off into space?"

The question fascinated Isaac as much as anyone. One day, it is said, while Isaac was in the family orchard, he saw an apple fall. He began to see some light on the mystery. He realized that everything in the universe has gravity. That means that every object pulls on every other object. Gravity is a very weak force compared to, say, magnetism. It takes the whole earth to pull on a big man with the force of even two hundred pounds. Imagine how little gravity the man's body itself has. Nevertheless, Isaac believed, gravity explains many things that we observe in the universe. The force that pulls a falling apple to the ground is the same force that pulls the moon out of a straight line, as if it were on a string, and keeps it swinging around the earth.

To prove it, Isaac considered the size of the moon, the size of the earth, and the distance they are away from each other. He calculated how far out of line the moon should curve every minute. His figures came close, but something did not quite hold true. So Isaac laid the puzzle aside for the time being.

After the plague, Isaac went back to the university and was accepted as a teacher. He had time to read, do experiments, and write. His work at the university helped to prepare him for one of his greatest projects. At the urging of a friend, Edmund Halley, he undertook to write a book explaining some of the things he had discovered. He began his work in 1685.

While he was writing, he was very much absorbed in his project. Sometimes when he woke in the morning, he would sit on the edge of his bed in his nightclothes, thinking and writing. Many times he would forget to eat food that was brought to him because he was thinking of something much more interesting. He worked sixteen to eighteen hours a day. It was an exhausting project.

Isaac called his book (three books, really) *Principia*. This means "principles." Isaac was interested in the principles that

Isaac Newton...

made things work. For example, he explained the three laws of motion. In our own words, these principles are as follow:

1. *A non-moving object stays still until something moves it.* You can jerk a placemat out from under a dish on a table (if you do it right!) because the non-moving dish tends to remain non-moving. By the same token, *a moving object continues moving in a straight line unless something interferes with its motion.* In other words, a thrown ball will slow down and curve back down to earth because the resistance of air and the force of gravity interfere with its motion. But the moon flies on and on, because nothing works against it.

2. *The change in motion of a body depends upon the mass of the body and the force acting upon it.* The more heavily you load a wagon, the harder it will be for you to pull it because the mass of the wagon increases.

3. *For every action, there is an equal and opposite reaction.* When a gun is fired, the bullet flies one way and the gun kicks in the other. By the same principle, a rocket "fires" exhaust gas one way and flies in the other.

Isaac Newton said that these three laws of motion, along with the law of gravity, could explain every movement of the sun, moon, and stars. By this time, Isaac had learned why the numbers did not hold true earlier when he had tried to calculate the path of the moon. The earth's size is different from the size he had figured.

One of the toughest subjects Isaac ever puzzled over was the matter of tides. People had guessed that the gravity of the moon affected the tides, but they could not understand why tides are much higher in some places than others, or why tides at a particular place are sometimes extra high or extra low. Maybe the moon had nothing to do with it after all? Isaac explained that, yes, the moon's gravity affected the tides, but so did the friction of the ocean floor, delaying the tides. So did the sun's gravity, sometimes working along with the moon's gravity and sometimes against it. Other factors affected the tides too.

Newton was displeased when he learned that after some people had read *Principia*, they had gotten the idea that the universe is basically just a giant clock. It was so much more than that! Isaac believed that to study nature was to understand God better. In his second edition of *Principia*, Newton wrote pointedly, "This most beautiful system of the sun, planets, and comets could only proceed from the counsel and dominion of an intelligent and powerful Being."

Isaac wrote a book called *Opticks,* in which he showed with diagrams how he had experimented with prisms, breaking sunlight into a rainbow of colors, and then using another prism to change the rainbow back into white light. White, he concluded, is not the absence of color, but a combination of all the colors. But he did not pretend to know everything about light. In the back of the book, he listed some problems he had not yet solved.

But the subject that fascinated Isaac the most was theology—the study of God Himself. Ever since boyhood, he had

Isaac Newton...

spent much time with the Bible. In manhood, he not only read the Bible but also took many notes on it, enough to fill several good-sized books. In fact, he wrote a few religious books, one of which was called *Observations on the Prophecy of Daniel and the Apocalypse of St. John.* Newton said he thought the Bible gives us prophecies, not so that we can guess about the future, but so that we can recognize when prophecies are fulfilled. Newton did not join the Church of England because he believed that some of its doctrines did not fit the Bible he had studied.

Isaac hated to get into arguments with people. His friends had to plead with him to publish his discoveries, for he knew other scientists would challenge what he had to say. He said, "I see a man must either be resolved to put out nothing new, or to become a slave to defend it." In spite of some arguments that his writings caused, Isaac became well respected. In fact, a poet named Alexander Pope paid him a very high compliment:

> Nature and Nature's laws lay hid in night:
> God said, "Let Newton be!" And all was light.

It would be difficult to list all of Newton's accomplishments. He invented a good reflecting telescope. He opened a new branch of mathematics called calculus. Newton served the government for some years as master of coinage, and he also sat in Parliament. Although he worked in Parliament behind the scenes, in the Assembly he had little to say. Once, and only once, did he rise to speak, and that was to ask that a window be closed because of a draft.

... A Dreamer Who Made Good

Although many people think Isaac Newton was the greatest mathematician and scientist who ever lived, Newton kept a modest opinion of himself. He said, "I do not know what I may appear to the world, but to myself I seem to have been only like a boy playing on the seashore, and diverting myself in now and then finding a smoother pebble or a prettier shell than ordinary, whilst the great ocean of truth lay all undiscovered before me."

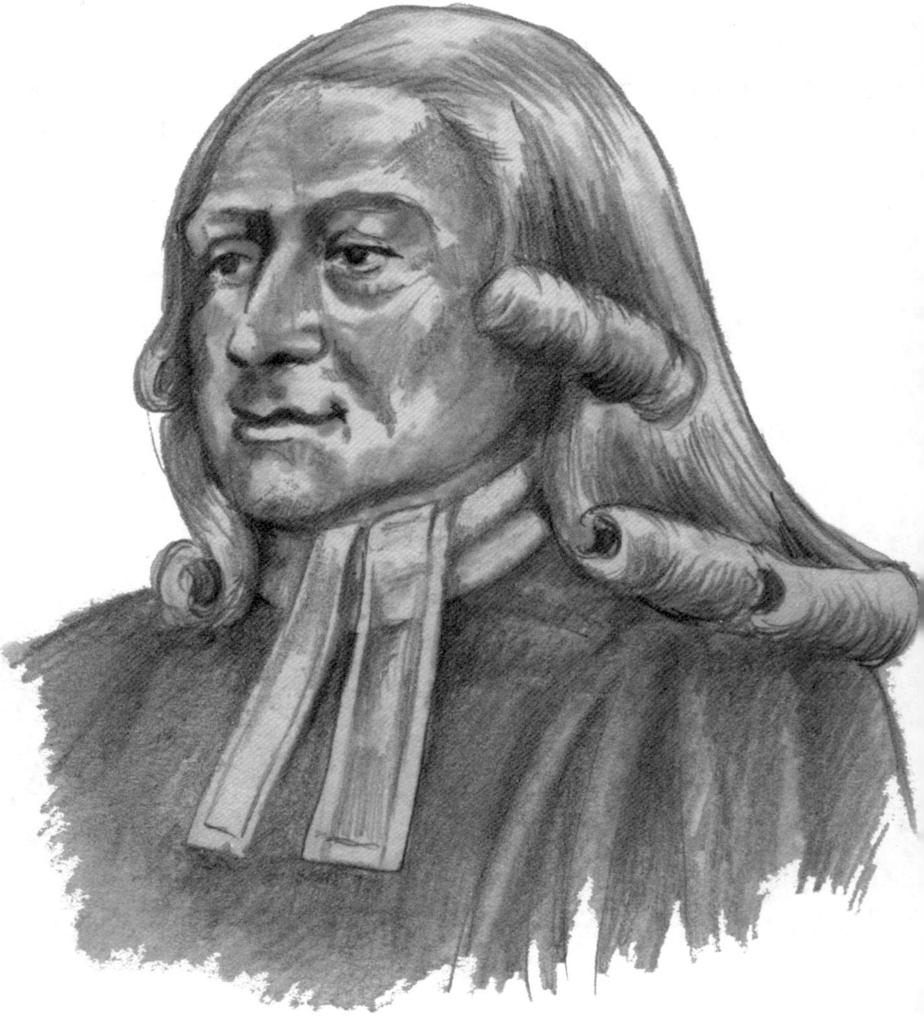

JOHN WESLEY

THE METHODIST MOVEMENT IS BORN

(AD 1703–1791)

England in 1703 was no country that you would choose to live in. The people knew little about the Bible and less about how Jesus Christ could transform them into godly people. Many of them were ill-mannered, dirty, and brutal.

Was the church a light to the people? Too often it was not. Ministers themselves were drinking and playing cards instead of preaching the Gospel, visiting the people, and reaching out to the lost. Their sermons were dry because they knew little of the Lord.

John was born into a big family, the fifteenth of nineteen children. Eight of the children died in infancy; this home must have had many sorrows. But John's mother, Susannah, did the best she could. Every week, she spent an hour individually with

JOHN WESLEY...

each of her children in religious conversation and prayer. John's hour with her came on Thursday evening.

John's father was Samuel Wesley, a poorly paid pastor. Not everyone liked Samuel's plain preaching. Local toughs (likely) set fire to the house twice. The second time, no one could stop the fire, and the family hurried to escape. Outside, they realized that six-year-old John, who had been sleeping upstairs, was not with them. Suddenly they saw him looking from a window. One neighbor stood on the shoulders of another and pulled him out just as the roof fell in. John never forgot his narrow escape and thought of himself as a "brand plucked from the burning."

When John was seventeen, he entered the famous Oxford University. He, his younger brother Charles, and several others met regularly to encourage each other in living godly lives. They prayed often, studied the Bible, fasted twice a week from morning until three in the afternoon, and took Communion every Sunday. They visited the sick, the poor, and even the miserable jails of that time. Other students laughed at the "Holy Club" and their methodical ways, calling them "method-ists." Indeed, the students in the Holy Club had to learn over time not to be so hard on themselves that they became sick.

In those days, men could be thrown into prison for small crimes or even if they could not pay off their debts on time. General James Oglethorpe thought he knew of a better way to treat these people. He founded a colony in Georgia where people could have a chance to start over again. He invited John and Charles to visit Georgia.

. . . The Methodist Movement Is Born

That voyage on a little ship was an education for John. When a storm came up and waves came pouring across the deck, some of the passengers screamed. John and Charles were frightened, but a group of religious people on board, called Moravians, kept on singing!

In Georgia, things did not go well for John. The people he preached to did not like his religion, which seemed too full of self-persecution. In fact, God Himself seemed far away. When he discussed matters with a Moravian preacher, the man came right to the point. "Do you know Jesus Christ?" John replied, "I know he is the Saviour of the world." The minister said, "True, but do you know He saves you?" John finally said he did, but later he wrote, "I fear they were mere words."

Back in England, still troubled, John went to a prayer meeting where he finally found the peace he was looking for. "About a quarter before nine, while I was listening to Luther's description of the change which God works in the heart through faith in Christ, I felt my heart strangely warmed. I felt I did trust in Christ, Christ alone, for salvation; and an assurance was given me, that He had taken away my sins, even mine, and saved me from the law of sin and death."

John did not join the Moravians. He stayed with the Church of England, but he stirred it from within. He began preaching about how Jesus Christ saves from sin. His message warmed many hearts. But people who had been settled church members all their lives did not like to be unsettled. John found church doors closed to him.

John Wesley ...

A friend of John named George Whitefield suggested the answer: If you cannot preach inside a church, why not preach outside? At first John thought this did not sound very religious, but then he remembered that Jesus preached in the open air. John learned that he could preach in fields and on street corners. He preached to miners and factory workers—people who had not been interested in the church because the church had not been interested in them. His brother Charles and his friend George Whitefield also preached, sometimes to ten, twenty, thirty thousand or more people at a time.

Church leaders told Wesley to stick to his own parish, as other ministers did. Wesley replied, "The world is my parish." On horseback, in heat or cold, he traveled across England, Scotland, Wales, and Ireland, preaching the Gospel.

John Wesley did more than preach. He organized little "societies" of people who worshiped together and encouraged each other in godliness. Some of these "Methodists" were beaten or were fired from their jobs. Some of them had their houses burned down. Mobs threatened Wesley himself. But the movement went on.

Wesley was a bookworm. He did most of his reading with his book propped on the pommel of his saddle, for he often rode fifty miles in a day and sometimes ninety. He read through books on science, history, medicine, and various other subjects. He urged his fellow ministers also to do much reading.[14]

---

14 Robert J. Morgan, *Nelson's Complete Book of Stories, Illustrations, and Quotes* (Nashville, TN: Thomas Nelson Publishers, 2000), p. 659

. . . The Methodist Movement Is Born

John's brother Charles did a work that in some ways lasted longer than John's. He wrote songs—some six thousand of them. Sometimes after composing a poem on horseback, he would ask someone for a pen and paper so he could write it down. We still sing songs such as "Jesus, Lover of My Soul" and "Love Divine, All Loves Excelling."

After Wesley died, his followers withdrew from the Church of England and formed the Methodist Church. By then, England was quite different from what it had been when he was born. Homes had become peaceable. Towns had less crime. People who had never belonged to any church were now Christians. Churches had a new zeal for evangelism. But Wesley did not take the credit to himself. He often said, "This is not my work. This is what Jesus Christ can do in a man's heart."

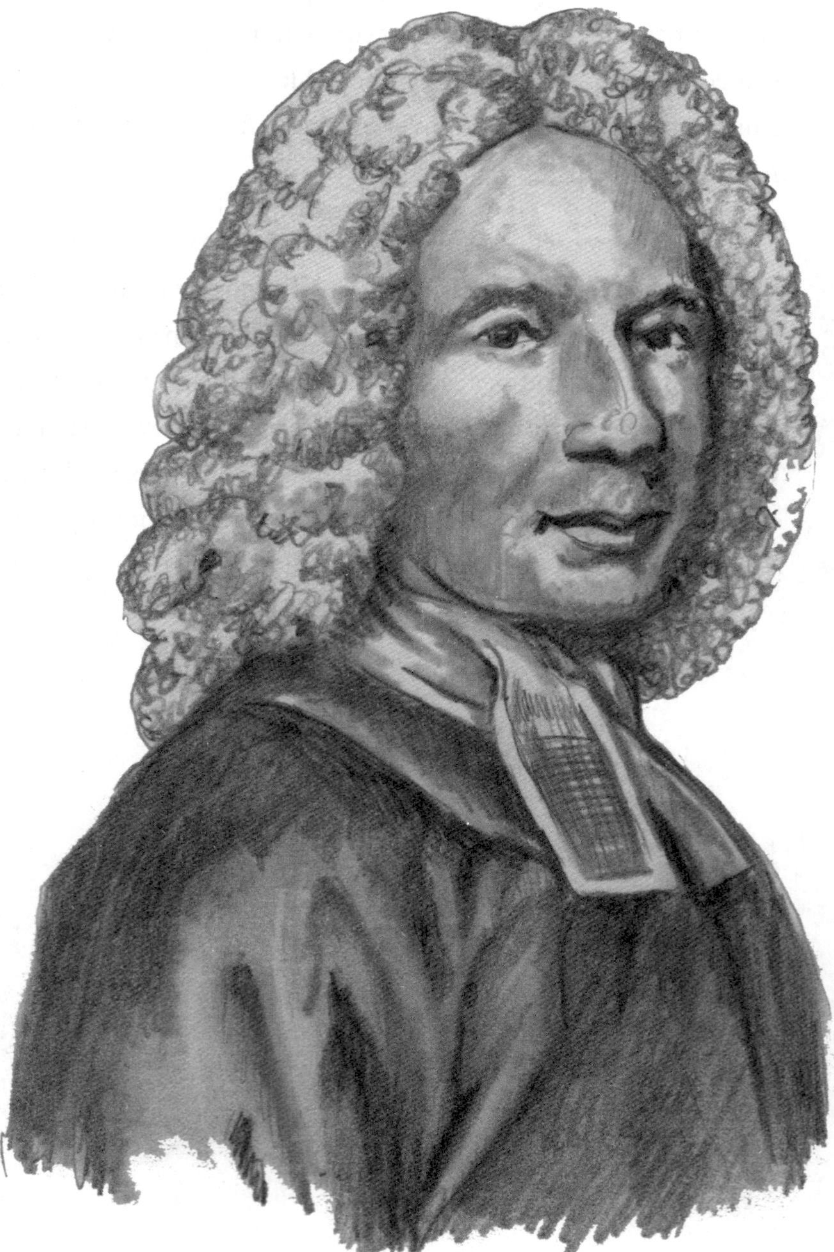

Isaac Watts

Father of English Hymnody

(AD 1674–1748)

People like to tell stories about Isaac Watts. As a boy, Isaac made up rhymes on the spot. Once he laughed during family devotions, and his father asked him why. Isaac replied, "A mouse for want of better stairs ran up a rope to say his prayers."

One day, after having put up with Isaac's many rhymes for years, his father threatened to punish him if he did not quit it. Before Isaac thought to stop himself, he said, "Oh, Father, do some pity take, and I will no more verses make."

Isaac's family belonged, not to the established Church of England, but to a dissenting church. (Three times Isaac's father was locked in the city jail.) However, some things about this new church were old. The group kept singing paraphrased Psalms, and Isaac wished for a wider selection. He complained until his father said, "Give us something better, young man."

Isaac Watts...

So Isaac took up the challenge. The next Sunday, he had prepared a new song for the congregation. It began, "Behold the glories of the Lamb / Amid the Father's throne / Prepare new honors for His name / And songs before unknown." The congregation obligingly sang this song "before unknown" and decided they liked its simple, worshipful style. Isaac continued to prepare a new song for the congregation each week. By 1707, he had enough songs to make a book simply called *Hymns*. In all, Watts wrote more than seven hundred psalms and hymns.

Often Watts used a psalm as an inspiration for his poetry. For instance, "O God, Our Help in Ages Past" is based on Psalm 90. A hymnbook he published in 1719 is called *The Psalms of David Imitated in the Language of the New Testament*. But the fact that he felt free to depart from the Psalms, as in "Alas! And Did My Saviour Bleed," was something new. Watts has been called the father of English hymnody.

You may have noticed that people who create beauty, whether musicians, woodworkers, gardeners, or poets, are not always beautiful themselves. Isaac was sickly all his life, and his head looked too big for his body. A woman he would have liked to marry declined, gently explaining that she liked the gem inside the casket, but. . . . He never married.

Not everyone approved of Watts's poetry, even long after he died. In 1789, at a general assembly of the Presbyterian Church in Philadelphia, a minister said to the group, "I have ridden on horseback all the way from my home in Kentucky to ask this august body to refuse to allow the great and pernicious error of adopting the use of Isaac Watts's hymns in public worship in preference to Rouse's versifications of the Psalms of David."[15]

Was Watts anything other than a poet? Actually, he was quite a successful minister. He wrote a number of books as well, on subjects as varied as astronomy, geography, and English grammar. But his hymns are what we remember him by. His three best known are "O God, Our Help in Ages Past," "When I Survey the Wondrous Cross," and "Joy to the World!" Worshipers will be singing these, and many other of Watts's hymns, to the end of time. Few men in history have guided the thinking of more people, more frequently.

---

[15] Clint Bonner, *A Hymn Is Born* (Nashville, TN: Broadman, 1959), p. 8, and Ernest K. Emurian, *Living Stories of Famous Hymns* (Grand Rapids, MI: Baker Book house, 1955), p. 17, cited in Morgan, p. 94.

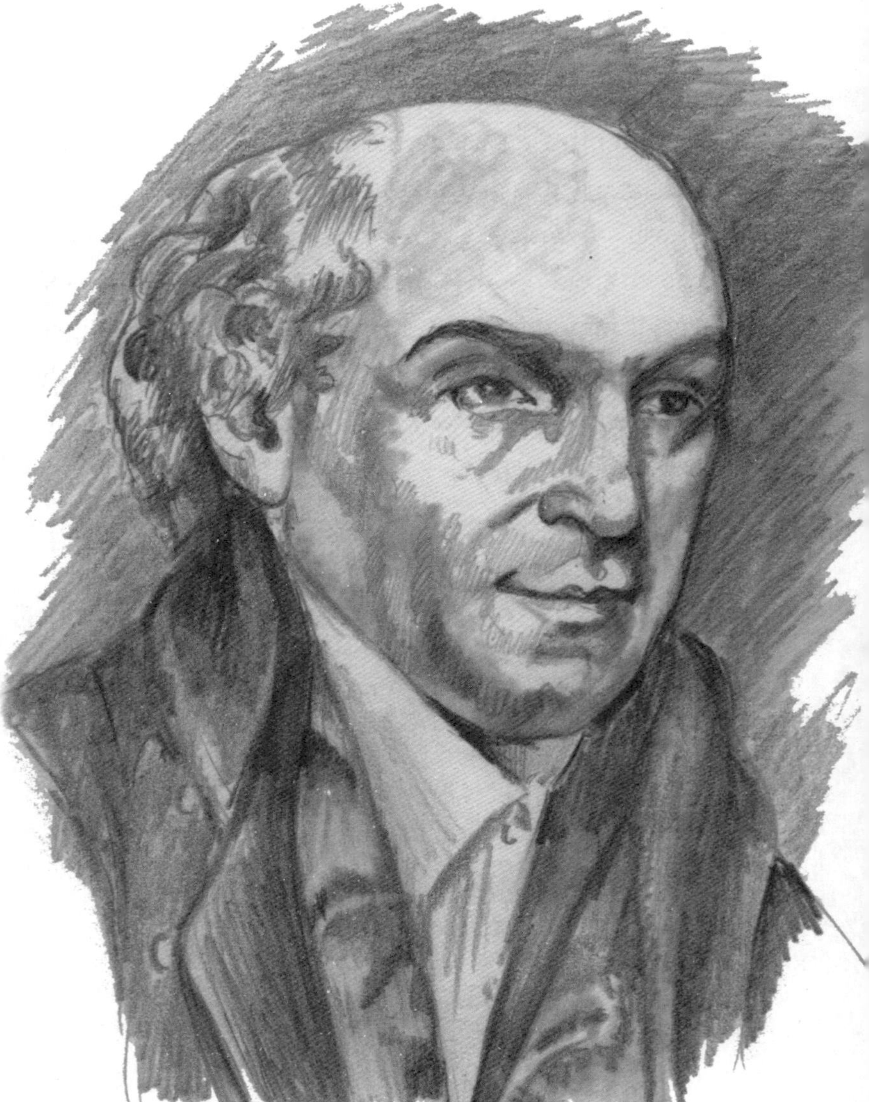

WILLIAM CAREY

Father of Modern Missions

(AD 1761–1834)

While George Washington was struggling through the American Revolution, William Carey was a young man in England. He became a shoemaker[16] but wanted to do more with his life, so he urged other Christians to start a mission in foreign countries. He brought up the subject so often that others grew tired of it. Once in a meeting, an older minister said, "Young man, sit down! When God pleases to convert the heathen, He'll do it without consulting you or me."

---

16 Note: It is not perfectly clear that Carey was a shoemaker. "There is a story told of Carey, the great missionary, that he was invited by the Governor-General of India to go to a dinner party at which were some military officers belonging to the aristocracy, and who looked down upon the missionaries with scorn and contempt.

"One of those officers said at the table, 'I believe that Carey was a shoemaker, wasn't he, before he took up the profession of a missionary?'

"Mr. Carey spoke up and said, 'Oh, no, I was only a cobbler. I could mend shoes, and wasn't ashamed of it.'"

—D. L. Moody, *Moody's Anecdotes* (Chicago, IL: The Bible Institute Colportage Association, 1898), pp. 92–93

Disappointed but not daunted, William wrote a book on the subject. Later he had the opportunity to preach a sermon at a Baptist convention. Once again, he urged the church to go into missions. He told his audience, in words often quoted today, "Attempt great things for God, expect great things from God." But the following day during business meeting, no one seemed ready to act. Carey gripped the arm of a fellow minister named Andrew Fuller, saying, "Is nothing again going to be done?" Finally Fuller spoke up, recommending that someone prepare a plan to start a missionary society. They could look at this plan at their next meeting.

Five months later, fourteen men got together, drew up a plan, and took their first collection of pledges to support the mission work. William's dream was coming true. If they supplied the money, he would supply himself. In 1793, William and his little family set sail for India. William would never return, not even for a furlough.

Today, when airplanes whisk people to nearly any place in the world in a day or two, it is hard to imagine the Carey family sailing for five months, often through stormy weather. But William did not sit idle. He talked to others on the ship and learned some of the language of Bengal, the part of India where they were going.

Finally arriving, William and his family slipped quietly into a village where William could translate the Bible into Bengali. He had studied Greek and Latin when he was young, so he could translate straight from Greek. But although he had a talent for languages, who has a talent for grieving when his son dies, or when his wife becomes mentally ill, or when no one responds to his Gospel message?

Furthermore, William's whole work came into danger when agents of the East India Company found him. The Company did not like Christian missionaries. William was bringing a message of freedom, and the Company preferred to keep the Indians under their thumb. They gave William a choice: get out, or make yourself useful by working for us.

So William took a job supervising an indigo factory. This turned out to be a good thing, for it gave him a source of income. He could show the workers kindness, which was more than they received from other Englishmen. And he could talk with them and learn more Bengali.

The East India Company men were still not satisfied. They noticed William setting up a press so he could print his newly translated New Testament. Once again they gave him a choice: Give up your dreams of printing the New Testament, or give up your job and the income it provides. Either way, William's purposes would be destroyed.

But the Lord was watching. Just in time, William received good news. Other missionaries were coming! Soon came a young man William faintly remembered from England—William Ward, with Joshua Marshmann and his wife. They sized up the predicament William was in, and together they made plans. They would move, as the East India Company insisted, but not very far. Just seventeen miles away from Calcutta was Serampore, which was under Danish authority. On January 1, 1800, the missionary party slipped away and started to make a new home there. Marshmann and his wife set up a boarding school for European children, in order to provide an income for all.

The work of translation went fast. There were plenty of reasons to work hard, for the Indian people's needs were heartbreaking. Besides worshiping idols, they threw babies into the Ganges, their sacred river. When a man died and his body was burned, they would put his widow on the pyre, hold her down with poles, pour butter over everything, and set fire to it. This practice was called *suttee*. William spoke out against these practices.

One evening in 1813 came the dreaded call, "Fire!" Workers ran around the printshop shutting windows and doors. Then, like a good professional fireman, Ward hacked a hole in the roof and began trying to douse the flames. Workers kept bringing water, and the fight against the fire might have succeeded except someone, not understanding the science of firefighting, opened a downstairs window to throw water on the fire. Provided with fresh oxygen, the flames leaped up again, and the battle was lost. Workers managed to drag out the presses, but the priceless manuscripts, over which William and his friends had labored for the past three years, were burned.

Now what? William and his friends sent word home, "We are cast down, but not in despair. . . . Traveling a road the second time is usually done with greater ease and certainty. . . . We shall improve the translations lost."

Shocked by news of the fire, Christians in England quickly sent so much money that the mission could rebuild. Volunteers offered to come and help. William and his friends sat down to redo their work. By 1832, William Carey and his fellow missionaries had translated, or helped to translate, at least part of the Bible into forty-four Indian languages.

When William Carey died in 1834, the flags of British India flew at half-mast. Under Christian influence, throwing babies into the river and burning widows was no longer acceptable in India. Today Carey is known as the Father of Modern Missions. But Carey had never been minded to draw attention to himself. He said, "After I am gone, please speak not of Dr. Carey, but rather of my wonderful Saviour."

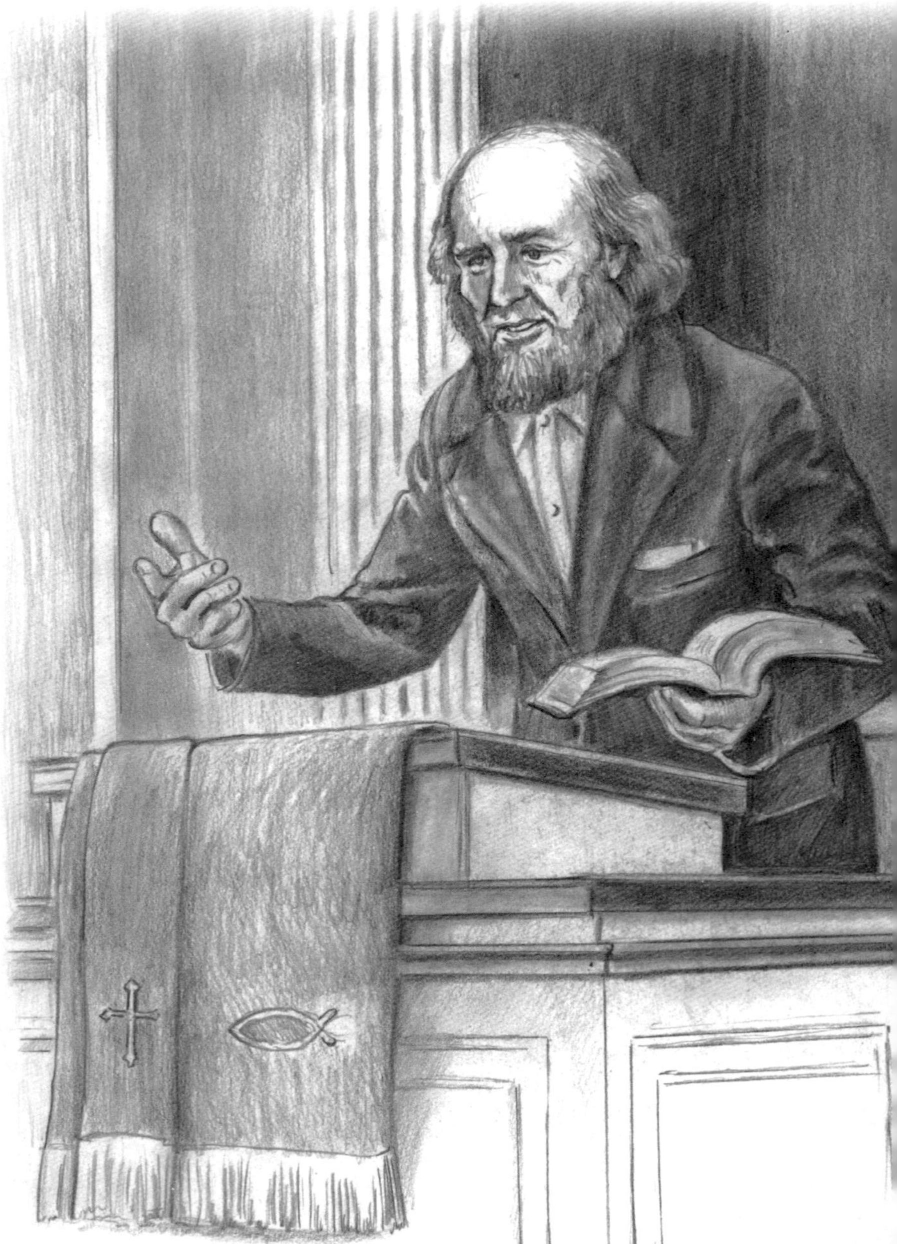

CHARLES FINNEY

LAWYER TURNED EVANGELIST

(AD 1792–1875)

Many people loved Charles Finney; many people hated him. Once a man who highly disapproved of Finney was told by his doctor that he was dying, and if he had something to say, he had better say it quick. The man managed to say, "Don't let Finney pray over my corpse!"

Charles Finney grew up in the backwoods of western New York State. He had only basic schooling and knew little about religion, for his parents were not Christians. But when he became a young man, he improved his education, studying Latin, Greek, and Hebrew. Deciding to become a lawyer, he studied law in the office of an older lawyer called Squire Wright.

Charles had noticed that many times his law books referred to the Bible, so he decided to find out for himself what the Bible said. He bought a Bible, the first one he had ever owned, and

Charles Finney...

found it interesting. But he was embarrassed to be seen studying it, so whenever someone walked into his office, he would put his law books on top of it.

Charles attended church and learned to know the preacher, who would sometimes drop in at his office to talk. Charles disagreed with the preacher on many points, and this led him to study the Bible more carefully. However, when someone asked if he would like to be prayed for, he retorted, "I do not see that it will do much good, for you have been praying for revival for years and do not have it yet."

Nevertheless, the Word of God kept working its way into his heart. Trained in a lawyer's way of thinking, Charles realized that the Bible made sense. Finally, he had to ask himself, "Since the Bible is true, what am I going to do about it?"

He began to pray. Afraid of being caught praying, he stopped the keyhole of the door and prayed only in a whisper. The conviction of sin became heavier. His vision of Christ on the cross became more compelling.

At last, one morning as he was walking to work, he kept on walking clear out of the village to a woods to be alone with God. He found a spot among several fallen trees and tried to pray—and couldn't! He was desperate. He had made up his mind not to leave the spot until he had found peace with God, but how was he to find it?

All the while, he was afraid someone would happen by and see him there praying. Finally he realized that his own pride was coming between him and God. When he cried out in shame at the thought of his sin, the Lord touched him with peace. After some time with the Lord, pondering His promises and praying, Charles left his nook among the trees and walked back into the village. "So perfectly quiet was my mind that it seemed as if all nature listened," he said afterward. He had been in the woods for hours—from early morning until noon—and had not realized it.

That first evening, Charles had another encounter with the Lord. He wrote of it later, "Without any expectation of it, without ever having the thought in my mind that there was any such thing for me, without any recollection that I had ever heard the thing mentioned by any person in the world, the Holy Ghost descended on me in a manner that seemed to go through me, body and soul.... No words can express the wonderful love that was shed abroad in my heart. I wept aloud with joy and love."[17]

The next morning, when he was back in his office, the older lawyer walked in. Charles said a few words to him about his need to give his heart to the Lord. The other lawyer just hung his head and walked out, but Charles's arrow had found its way to his heart. Later the older man did turn his life over to the Lord.

Charles had always enjoyed legal work, but now he found a new love, winning souls for the Lord. That day he began talking to people about their need for salvation. The news spread that Charles Finney had been converted. That evening, Finney went

---

[17] James Gilchrist Lawson, *Deeper Experiences of Famous Christians* (Anderson, IN: Warner Press, 1911), p. 180.

Charles Finney...

to church, even though no service had been announced, and found that most of the villagers had come to hear him speak! That was the first of a series of meetings when many people got right with the Lord.

Not everyone liked Charles Finney's way of speaking. He was forceful and earnest and had a way of putting people on the spot. Either they had repented or they had not, and what were they going to do about it? When Finney first told an audience the story of his own conversion, a lawyer walked out, saying, "He is in earnest, but he is deranged."

One time when Finney was visiting a community, he chose to preach about Lot being rescued from Sodom. It so happened that the community was commonly called Sodom, and a good man living there was called Lot. The people thought Finney was deliberately talking about them. They were furious. But a strange conviction fell upon them, and they began to drop to their knees, calling on God for mercy. Finney remarked, "If I had had a sword in both hands, I could not have cut them down as fast as they fell."

Charles Finney traveled far on his preaching campaigns, even to Europe. It is difficult to say how many people responded to the call of Christ because of his ministry, but we may safely guess hundreds of thousands did. Even more remarkable, researchers found that over eighty-five percent of the people who were converted under Finney's teaching were still following Christ years later. Very few other evangelists have done as well. Perhaps

... Lawyer Turned Evangelist

one reason for this was that Finney insisted that people do more than become converted—they must live holy lives ever after.[18]

Charles Finney helped to found Oberlin College in Ohio and served as its first president. The college enrolled both black and white students, in years when this was unusual. The influence of the college helped to turn people's minds against slavery. As Finney grew old, he could no longer go on preaching tours, but he continued to teach theology at Oberlin.

What was Finney's secret of winning souls? There was no secret. He wrote several books explaining how to succeed in evangelism. If anything summed it up, it would be his comment, "A revival is nothing else than a new beginning of obedience to God."[19]

---

18 Lawson, 175.
19 E.E. Shelhamer, ed., *Finney on Revival* (Minneapolis, MN: Bethany House Publishers), p. 7.

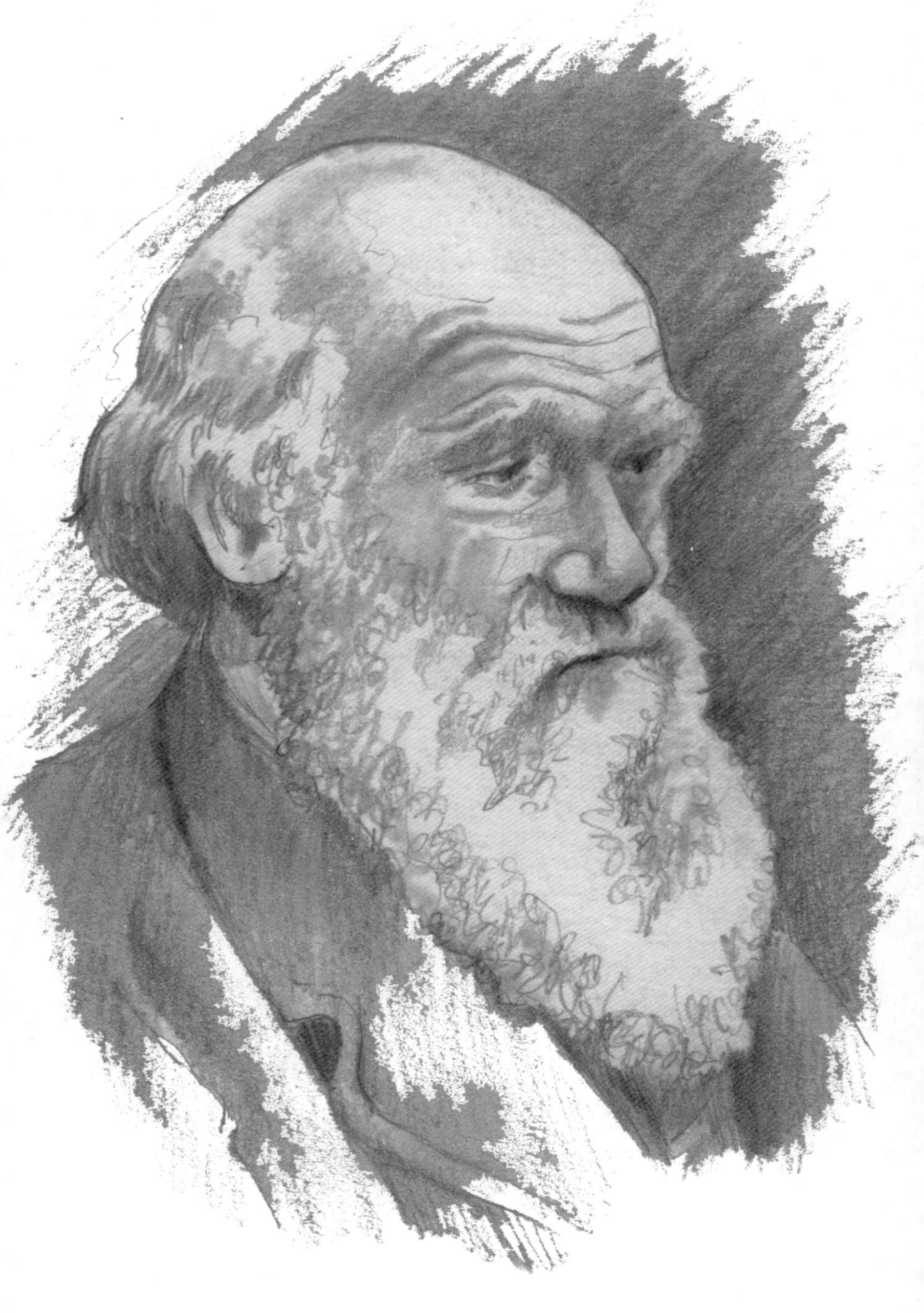

Charles Darwin

A Book That Argued for Evolution

(AD 1809–1882)

Charles Darwin was a man of his times. In other words, he thought along the same lines that other people of his times were thinking. Those were the days when scientists were making great discoveries, doctors were finding ways to help people live longer, and trains and telegraphs were helping people to travel and communicate faster. Many people were thinking that mankind had found the key to progress. Surely things would keep getting better and better! Darwin gave this kind of thinking a great boost when he wrote his most famous book, *On the Origin of Species*.

As a boy in England, Charles read a book his grandfather had written about the theory of evolution. Evolution was already an old, old idea. It was the belief that the many different kinds of living things we see today—anything from germs to giraffes to gentlemen—all belong to the same family tree. It taught that, millions of years ago, there were fewer kinds of creatures, and they were more simple in their design; many more millions of years ago, there was only one kind. A very simple form of life, something like pond scum, became the ancestor of us all. This, of course, is quite different from the Creation that the Bible describes. Charles learned about the Bible, but he never forgot the discussions he had heard about evolution.

In young manhood, Charles studied to be a doctor, and then to be a minister. Being a nature lover, Charles also rambled in fields and woods and collected specimens—especially of beetles. He wrote, "One day, while tearing off some old bark, I saw two rare beetles, and seized one in each hand; then I saw a third and new kind, which I could not bear to lose, so that I popped the one which I held in my right hand into my mouth. Alas! it ejected some intensely acrid fluid, which burnt my tongue so that I was forced to spit the beetle out, which was lost, as was the third one."

Still, he loved nature, and his imagination really caught fire when he went on a five-year trip around the world with other scientists on a ship called the *Beagle*. It was his job to study plants and animals wherever he went. As he studied nature and collected specimens, he was struck by the thought that every animal is a little different from other animals like it. Usually these little differences do not matter. But sometimes an animal lives longer because it is a little stronger than its fellows or can see or hear a little better. This animal is likely to have offspring that are also stronger and more able to survive.

Darwin was right, up to that point. It is true that stronger creatures live longer and reproduce, whereas the weaker ones

. . . A Book That Argued for Evolution

die. But Darwin took his thinking a step further. He thought that over millions of years, not only would plants and animals remain strong and healthy generation after generation, but also that some of their offspring would turn into better and totally different kinds of plants and animals. In other words, pond scum might evolve into . . . water lilies. In fact, he thought, this was how all the different kinds of plants and animals came from just one. Evolution, to Darwin, made sense!

While Darwin was thinking about science, he was also thinking about God. His faith in God had been quite firm as a boy, and he had believed that God answered his prayers. But now as a man, he thought of questions about religion that he did not know how to answer. He wrote, "Thus disbelief crept over me at a very slow rate, but was at last complete. The rate was so slow that I felt no distress."[20] This did not mean Darwin completely threw away the idea of God. He wrote, "I for one must be content to remain an agnostic."[21] An agnostic believes that God is unknown or unknowable.

A few years after his trip on the *Beagle*, Darwin married, but also around this time, his health began to go downhill. One of his children wrote, "For nearly forty years he never knew one day of the health of ordinary men, and . . . his life was one long struggle against the weariness and strain of sickness." Again, "His nights were generally bad, and he often lay awake or sat up in bed for hours, suffering much discomfort."

---

20 Francis Darwin, ed., *The Autobiography of Charles Darwin and Selected Letters* (New York, NY: Dover Publications, 1958), p. 62.
21 Darwin, p. 66.

Charles Darwin...

It is not clear why Darwin chose to marry his cousin. Relatives who marry often have children with the weaknesses of their parents. Certainly Darwin was devoted to his wife, and he enjoyed playing with his children. (Once during his regular working hours, one of his little boys brought him sixpence, hoping to bribe his father to play with them.)[22] But in later years, Darwin regretfully wrote, "My life has been a very happy one; the greatest drawback being that several of my children have inherited from me feeble health."[23]

People criticized Darwin's book. One friend wrote in a long letter, "I have read your book with more pain than pleasure. Parts of it I admired greatly, parts I laughed at till my sides were almost sore; other parts I read with absolute sorrow, because I think them utterly false and grievously mischievous."[24] Some people who wrote to Darwin were less kind than this or even unreasonable, but Darwin tried to answer them all patiently.

Darwin had many interests besides evolution. For instance, he wrote two books on barnacles. In October of 1852 he wrote, "I am at work at the second volume of the Cirripedia [barnacles], of which creatures I am wonderfully tired. I hate a barnacle as no man ever did before, not even a sailor in a slow-sailing ship."[25]

During the last year of his life, Darwin was talking to the Duke of Argyll, who mentioned Darwin's book on orchids and another book on earthworms. The duke said it was impossible to think that these wonderful creatures had formed without a mind

---

22 Darwin, p. 91.
23 Darwin, p. 296.
24 Darwin, p. 40.
25 Adam Sedgwick, cited in Darwin, p. 229.

... A Book That Argued for Evolution

to form them. He wrote later, "I shall never forget Mr. Darwin's answer. He looked at me very hard and said, 'Well, that often comes over me with overwhelming force; but at other times,' and he shook his head vaguely, adding, 'it seems to go away.' "[26]

After Darwin died, more and more scientific evidence arose to show that *On the Origin of Species* was seriously wrong. For instance, more fossils were discovered—millions of them, in fact. But they do not show a gradual change from one form of life to another. They stay basically the same down through the years. An ancient fossil of a starfish looks very much like the starfish we find on beaches today. This problem with fossils is just one of many problems with evolution.

Encyclopedias and textbooks often talk as if evolution has been proved, that nearly all scientists believe in it, and that just a few crackpots do not. The fact is that a host of scientists object to evolution. Many books have been written pointing out the holes in the theory, and various books show that the Bible's account of Creation and the Flood explains the world we see today.

Photographs of Charles Darwin later in life show a bald, white-bearded man with prominent, thoughtful-looking eyebrows. He was about six feet tall but stooped. Darwin was an interesting man, a kindly father, and a courteous letter-writer. As a hardworking scientist, he was eager to collect and organize all the facts. But he became less and less sure that God is the greatest fact of all. This led Darwin and his followers into serious errors.

---

[26] Darwin, p. 69.

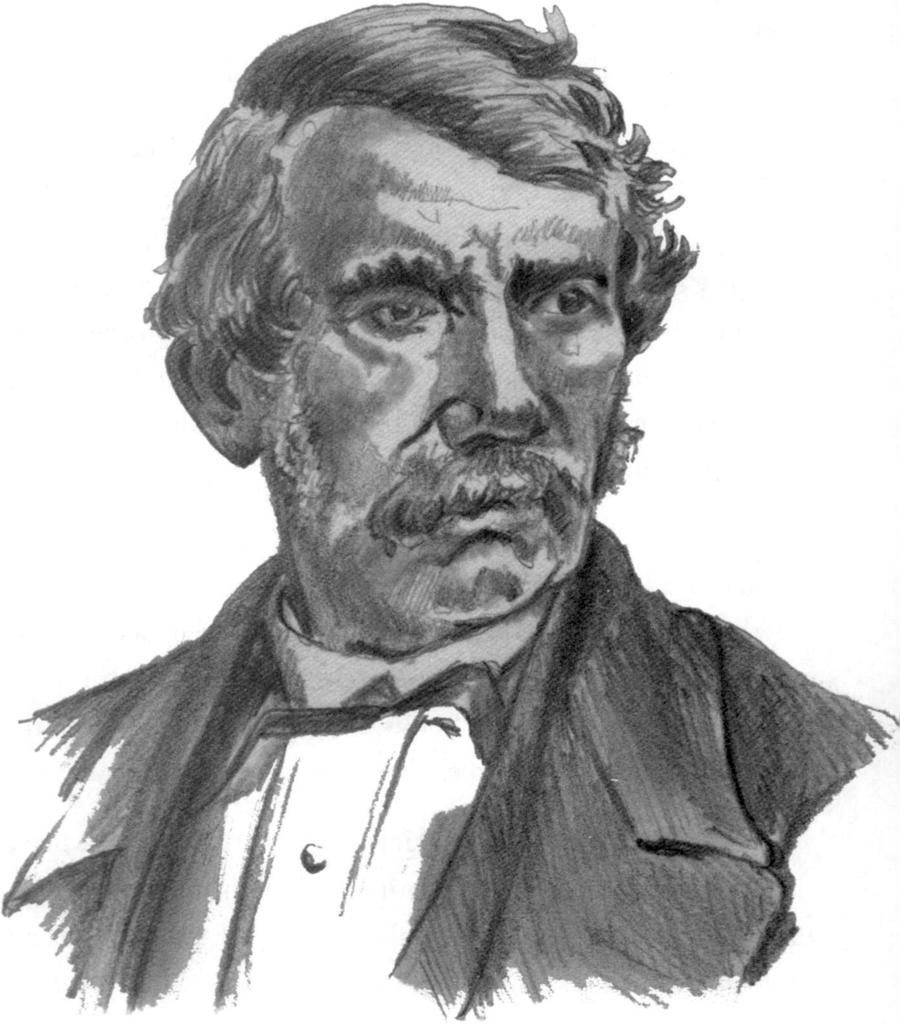

DAVID LIVINGSTONE

"I WILL OPEN A PATH THROUGH THE COUNTRY"

(AD 1813–1873)

A factory is not where you would go to study books, but in Scotland during the early 1800s, ten-year-old David Livingstone had no other choice. He was sent off to work in a textile factory, where he had to tend a loom. But with his first small earnings, he bought a Latin grammar book, propped it up near the loom, and snatched a little learning from it when he could.

When David became a young man, he read a letter sent to England from a missionary in China. Learning of the many needs there, David decided he wanted to serve in China too. Besides saving people's souls, he wanted to heal their bodies, so he studied to be a doctor. This was very expensive, but by saving his hard-won earnings and borrowing from his brother, he worked his way through.

David was not satisfied to educate his head; he educated his hands. He learned to do all sorts of odd jobs, which would come in handy later when he needed to do carpentry, cobble boots, and fix anything from wagons to pots and pans.

About the time David would have gone to China, one of the Opium Wars was raging there. So the London Missionary Society directed him to southern Africa instead. David was satisfied to change his plans, for he had heard missionary Robert Moffat say, "There is a vast plain to the north where I have sometimes seen in the morning sun the smoke of a thousand villages where no missionary has ever been." Soon after David arrived in southern Africa, he stayed in Robert Moffat's home. Later he married Moffat's daughter Mary.

At that time, maps of Africa showed its coastline, but people could only guess about its vast interior. North of the Moffats' home lay the Kalahari Desert. Did it extend into the heart of Africa? Was most of Africa desert? Not satisfied with his early journeys, David wanted to push farther into the continent and find out.

More than curiosity drove David. Once a twelve-year-old girl ran from slave traders and hid under David's wagon, bribing a trader away with the beads she wore. That was David's introduction to the slave trade. Later, he saw firsthand the smoldering villages that slave traders had burned, forcing the villagers to march to the coast where they would be shipped away as slaves.

... "I Will Open a Path Through the Country"

David determined to open up Africa to Christian missionaries and traders. He hoped this influence would help put an end to the slave trade. David said he would "open a path through the country, or perish."

David was a suitable man to explore the continent. On his voyage to Africa, David had learned from the ship's captain how to "shoot the sun" with a sextant. In this way, he could determine accurately how far north or south he was. It was much trickier to determine how far east or west he was. For that, he needed not only a sextant but also a very accurate clock, and all he had was his wind-up watch. Still, he did the best he could and carefully wrote up his records. David was also a great observer. He noted the birds and their calls, the trees, the flowers, the animals. He collected specimens and sent them to friends in England.

Before David could do much exploring, a lion living nearby became bold enough to start snatching animals in broad daylight. So David went with his African friends to try and kill it. When David saw the culprit, he fired both barrels. But the lion, instead of dying, pounced on David, shaking him the way a terrier shakes a rat. A native teacher fired at the lion, which then jumped on him. Then it turned on another man trying to kill it with a spear. But by then David's bullets had taken effect, and the lion dropped dead. David's upper arm was crushed. Even after it healed, the arm bore eleven tooth marks, and from then on he could not raise his arm without pain.

David and Mary had four children, but one of their children died, and David finally decided that Africa was not a healthy place for his family. With a leaden heart, he sent them home to England. In a farewell letter to his little girl Agnes, he wrote, "I shall not see you again for a long time, and I am very sorry."

The Kalahari was not so vast or desolate as the Sahara, but it was punishing enough. Everywhere, everywhere, soft white sand slowed the oxen's progress. And nowhere could David find water. Natives, however, knew there was water under the soil, which they drew up and stored in ostrich-egg shells. Once they found that Livingstone was their friend, they shared some water with him.

After David had finally crossed the Kalahari to Lake Ngami, he thought, "There must be a better way into Africa than from the south. Why not enter it from either the east or the west?" And so, in 1853, he set out from the interior to the west coast. Once he arrived at Luanda on the Atlantic, he made plans to retrace his steps partway and then to head across to the east coast.

David needed plenty of supplies for such a large journey. A chief whom David had befriended sent 114 baggage bearers with him. To keep good will with the African people, David would ask permission to cross their tribal territories. Some chiefs were suspicious, but usually David's reputation went before him, winning people's trust.

David had not forgotten that he was more than just an explorer who would open up Africa to missionaries. He was a missionary himself. With him he carried his "magic lantern," that would show pictures of Bible stories. This method helped him tell the people something of the Gospel message.

..."I Will Open a Path Through the Country"

On this trip, Africans told him about the "smoke that thunders." Finding his way along the Zambezi River, Livingstone at last came to one of the seven natural wonders of the world. The constant hissing, rumbling roar, the rainbow, the spray, and the mist rising two or three thousand feet high—all these impressed David deeply. He called it Victoria Falls, after his queen, Victoria. On a nearby tree, he carved his initials and the year—1855.

It was 1856 before David and his men saw the Indian Ocean ahead, and he knew he had opened a new way into Africa. By then it was high time to return to England, for he had been in Africa fifteen years in all. Visiting his family was high on his list.

On his next trip, beginning in 1858, David explored farther north, but still well south of the equator. The trip was very difficult, for he and his men had to "climb mountains, shoot rapids in a canoe, cross rocks so sunburnt that they scorched the feet of his native carriers." This time, with the help of a miserable, wheezing steamer that David called "The Asthmatic," David reached Lake Nyassa. The land here was at a high enough altitude that white men could live there in comfort.

On his last, and perhaps greatest, journey, beginning in 1866, David visited Lake Nyassa again, and then traveled on. Walking is good for the health, but walking under a burning sun, sometimes with a burning fever, or having to walk through rain so heavy that one has to carry his watch in his armpit to keep it dry, or having to wade through a river and pull off leeches afterward, is decidedly not good for the health. Then too, the hard corn he tried to eat broke his teeth. Still he pressed on, until most of his bearers grumbled and quit.

At last David arrived at Ujiji, on the shore of Lake Tanganyika. Here he could count on finding letters from home and new supplies. Well, he had *thought* he could. To his dismay, thieves had plundered everything. There was nothing to do but order more supplies from the coast and wait until they came. In his weak condition, David could do very little. During this time, he read the Bible through three times.

Unknown to him, the world had begun to worry about him. They had heard no word from him for several years. Was he dead? An American newspaper sent an Englishman named Henry Stanley to try and find him. In Africa, Stanley followed rumors and reports until he found his way to Ujiji. When they finally met, instead of exclaiming with excitement, Stanley fell back on the famously polite words, "Dr. Livingstone, I presume?" It was October 28, 1871. Stanley brought him mail, medicine, food, clothing, and his own friendship. David had not seen another white face for months.

When Stanley could not persuade Livingstone to return with him to England, he returned alone. Later, David began exploring once more, trying to discover the source of the Nile. This time, his energy drained rapidly. Thirteen months after Livingstone had said goodbye to Stanley, his comrades carried him into a village and built a hut for him. Two days later, his helpers saw him on his knees as if praying, and finally they realized he had died.

... "I Will Open a Path Through the Country"

They buried his heart in Africa but smuggled his body past hostile Arab slave traders to the coast. The 1500-mile trip took nearly a year. Then they shipped his body to England. Today it rests in Westminster Abbey with kings and queens and other noted people. On his tomb are written his own words, "May heaven's rich blessing come down on everyone, American, English, or Turk, who will help to heal this open sore of the world."

The "open sore" of which he spoke was slavery. David always hated slavery and spoke out against it. Partly through his influence, slavery gradually ended. However, because of his explorations and the explorations of others, European nations rushed to claim various parts of Africa for themselves. Britain, Portugal, France, Germany, and other nations claimed huge chunks. It turned out to be one of the biggest land grabs in history.

Still, the world admires David Livingstone because of his character and dedication. Then too, many missionaries followed him, as he had hoped, bringing the Gospel to people who had never heard it before. We remember Livingstone also for the motto that kept him going through all his loneliness and discouragements: "Lo, I am with you alway." He said that Jesus Christ was a gentleman of the highest honor, and He would not go back on His word.

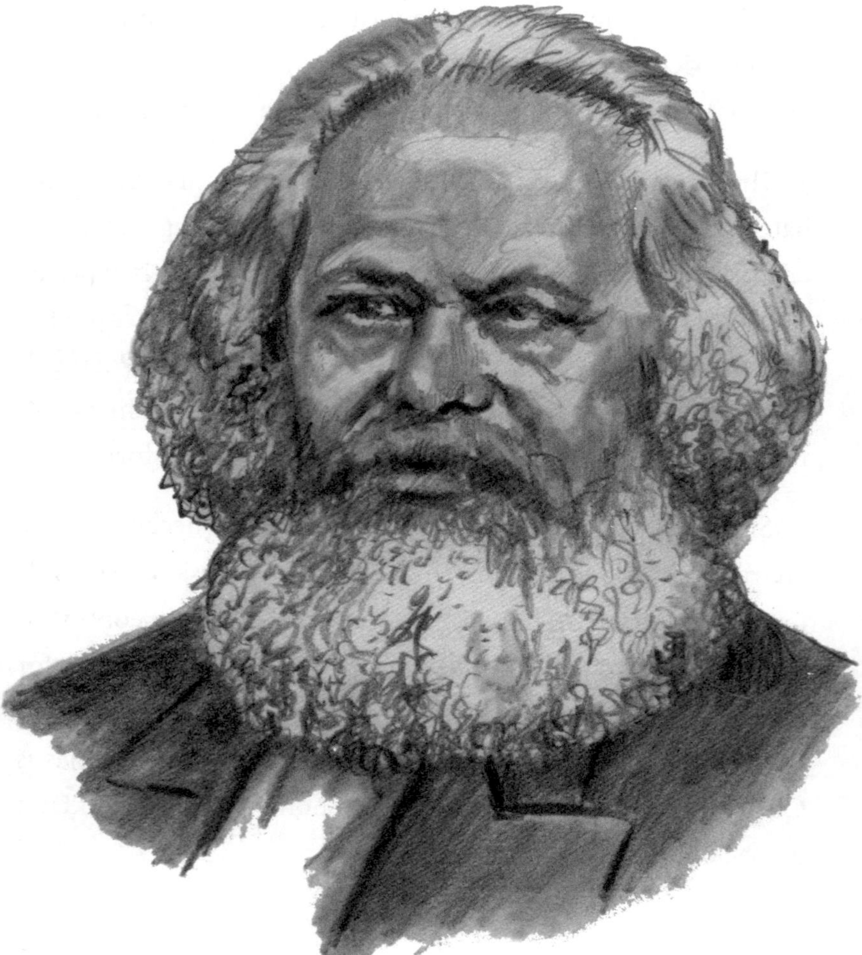

Karl Marx

Father of Communism

(AD 1818–1883)

Riddle: "What is fifty meters long and eats cabbage?" Answer: "A line of customers at a Russian butcher shop."

That was a good riddle in Russia when quality food was hard to get. It was also a strange riddle, for how could there be food shortages in a country with broad, fertile plains and huge farms? It happened because Russia had followed the advice of Karl Marx. His advice had ended up making the country poorer instead of richer.

Someone said that before you can understand a man, you must know his memories. This was true of Karl Marx. During the 1800s, he grew up in Prussia in what was later called Germany. Those were the days of the Industrial Revolution, when people worked long hours for little money. Even children worked in factories, and some were chained to their machines. For many people, it was a miserable time. Marx was troubled by this and wondered what could be done.

As a young man, Marx studied law for a while, but later he decided philosophy was more interesting. He became more than a philosopher—he was a radical and a revolutionary. He served as editor of several magazines that made sharp statements criticizing the way the country was run.

In 1848, Marx supported a revolution in Germany. When the revolution fell apart, he and his family fled to London and they lived there for the rest of his life. He spent most of his time in the royal library of England, studying and thinking. Often he did not feel well and suffered from depression.

Marx and an acquaintance named Friedrich Engels thought so much alike that they became fast friends. Together they worked on a small book called *The Communist Manifesto*. Engels gave Marx credit for its basic idea. Later they wrote a three-volume work called *Das Kapital*, which explained their ideas in more detail.

The Communist Manifesto was an angry book. It spoke about how people suffered, slaving away at their jobs without much to show for it. The book blamed the way things were set up, saying that the owners of factories and businesses paid their workers too little and kept too much of the profit for themselves. No doubt this was true.

But then Marx went further. He predicted that things would keep on getting worse until the workers would finally rise up and overthrow the business owners. Then the workers would own everything and share everything alike. Everyone would contribute what he could, and everyone would get what he needed. Communists looked for a future time when the government, police force, and army would "wither away" because there would be no need for them.

Marx had no time for religion. He called it the "opium" of the people because opium stupefies people and makes them content with things the way they are. Marx thought that religion stupefies people, that it makes them content with terrible injustices, because they are looking for heaven after this life. Marx wanted men to join the revolution of workers against their masters. The last line of *The Communist Manifesto* ran, "Workingmen of all countries, unite!"

Although Marx frowned on religion, what he offered his readers was a kind of religion of its own. Instead of God, he offered a kind of anti-God called atheism. Instead of church, he offered the Communist Party. Instead of Christian fellowship, he offered a fellowship of workingmen striving together to bring in a better world. Instead of heaven, he offered a utopia yet to come.

Although Marx and Engels went seriously off track in *The Communist Manifesto,* they wrote it so brilliantly that many readers were impressed. Engels and others thought Marx was the greatest thinker in the world. "Communism is the wave of the future," people said.

Where would the revolution start? Marx thought it would start in some industrialized country like Germany or England.

Karl Marx...

But a Communist named Nikolai Lenin thought otherwise. About twenty-four years after Marx died, Lenin started a revolution in Russia. When he died, Joseph Stalin carried it on.

Somehow the revolution did not work out the way Karl Marx had predicted. Certainly the Communists overthrew the government, but instead of moving on in a loving brotherhood of workingmen to set up the perfect community, the Communists destroyed many workingmen. They also fought among themselves. Stalin himself had old friends killed in bloody "purges" because he did not trust them. As the Communist movement spread to Eastern Europe, China, and other countries, the leaders of various countries quarreled bitterly among themselves.

Where had Marx gone wrong? He had made a number of mistakes, but the biggest one was that he had turned his readers loose from God. He had said that nothing is really wrong if it is done for the sake of Communism. His followers took him all too seriously. Telling a lie was just fine if it helped Communism. Killing people was right if they opposed Communism.

Marx's teachings spread from country to country until a third of the world had come under Communism. Wherever Communism went, Christians were oppressed, imprisoned, or tortured for their faith. Tens of thousands of churches were destroyed. Nevertheless, young people kept giving their hearts to the Lord, no matter what the cost. Christianity could not be destroyed.

As the years rolled on, more and more people in Russia and other Communist countries realized that Communism was not working. Around 1990, most Communist governments in

... Father of Communism

Europe gave up Communism. People chuckled and said, "The old saying has come true. Our Communist government has finally withered away!"

But in other countries, Communism remained. China was the biggest such country. Chinese leaders eventually moved away from the worst cruelties of the early Communists, but they still imprisoned Christians and severely limited the number of Bibles the people could own.

The world has paid a heavy price for Communism. Counting the man-made famines, the terrifying purges, and the persecutions, perhaps a hundred million people have lost their lives. That's a lot of uncles and aunts and cousins and parents and siblings and children and spouses.

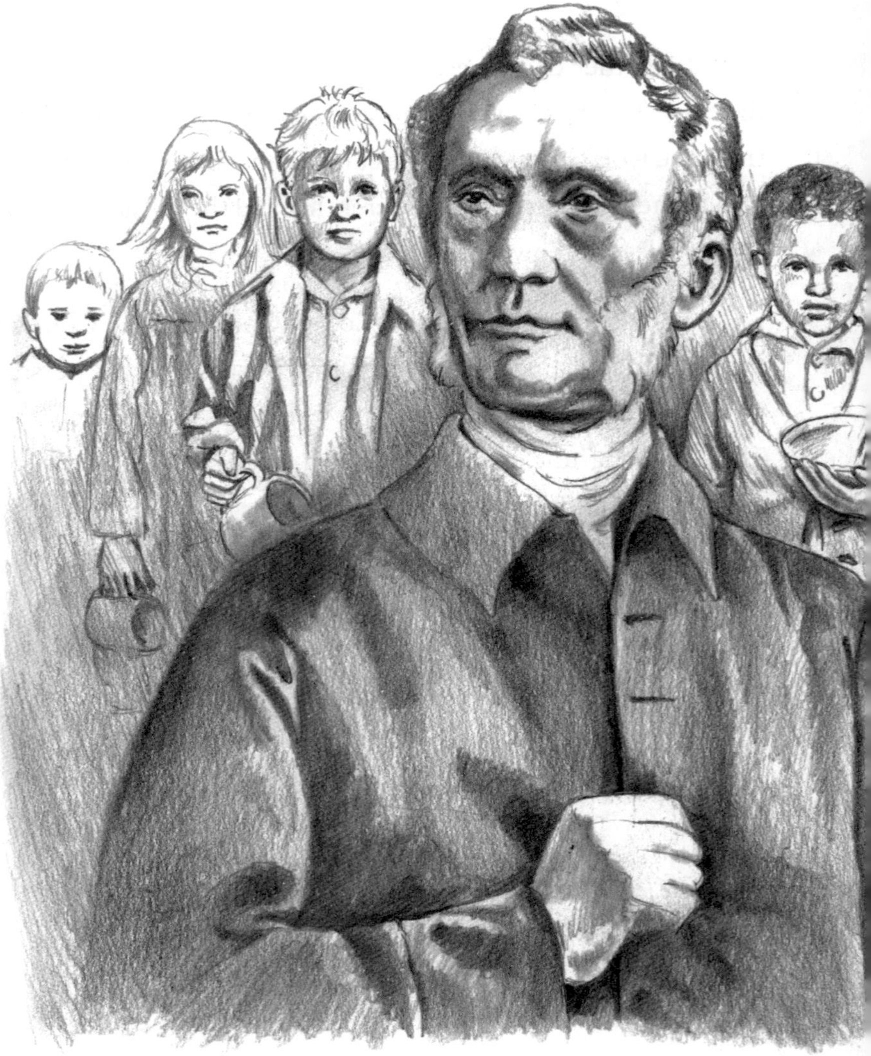

George Mueller

Quiet Faith in a Dependable God

(AD 1805–1898)

George was a German, though back in the days when he was a boy, there was no Germany as such. Like Karl Marx, he lived in a German land called Prussia. His father, who was a tax collector, did not know much about raising his son. He spoiled him by giving him what he wanted. George wrote later, "Before I was ten years old, I had repeatedly stolen government money which was entrusted to my father and forced him to make up the losses."[27] When George was sixteen, he landed in jail with other criminals. After a year, someone told George's father, who paid enough to get him out of jail but also "beat [him] severely."[28]

For a time, George pretended to reform. His school principal spoke of him highly. Yet although George claimed to be a Christian and took Communion regularly, he knew how rotten and

---
27 George Mueller, *Autobiography of George Mueller*, (Springdale, PA: Whitaker House, 1984), p. 10.
28 Mueller, p. 12.

sinful he was underneath. "I owned more than three hundred books," he wrote, "but no Bible."[29] He kept making resolutions to do better, and then kept falling back into sin.

But then he made a friend and attended one of his prayer meetings. The people at the prayer meeting, who simply called themselves the Brethren, had a very simple and sincere way of worshiping. They knelt to pray, something George had never seen before. And something about the way they prayed fascinated George. These people had a real contact with God! At age twenty, George, of all unlikely people, gave his heart to the Lord.

There was still much he did not know, but George determined to be as godly now as he had been ungodly before. However, when he shared his newfound joy with his father and asked his approval to be a missionary, his father was heartbroken! He told George he had invested a great amount of money in him so that when he got old, he could live with George in a comfortable parsonage. Now George was walking away from all that in order to be a missionary. When George heard that, he decided he would not accept any more money from his father. But the Lord provided him with a job teaching several Americans who did not understand German. George ended up with "enough money for school and some to spare."

After he moved to England in 1829, George served as pastor to a small congregation. The following year, he married Mary Groves. It is said that she was not very pretty, but that she was his faithful friend as long as she lived.

---

29 Mueller, p. 12.

... Quiet Faith in a Dependable God

About the time they married, George began to think he was getting his income the wrong way. People in his congregation would rent their pews, and he would collect the money and live on that. But he was troubled by the thought, "What if poor people have a hard time paying their rent? Besides, what if I preach less boldly because I am afraid to offend the people who pay me?" So he announced that he would no longer receive money from pew rents. Instead, he put up a box in the church with a little sign explaining that anyone who wanted to contribute to the ministry could do so. George never asked for money or even collected the money in the box himself.

During the following months, sometimes the Mueller household ran very low on money. Although George had asked the brethren to bring money from the offering box every week, sometimes it ran three, four, or five weeks before the money came. George would pray earnestly, and always, even at their lowest moments, someone would meet George, or drop in at the house, with a little money. At the end of a year, George found that he had received more than he would have under the old system. The Lord had blessed!

After moving to Bristol, George continued the same system, and finally he was able to write, "Four years have passed since I began to trust the Lord alone for the supply of my temporal needs.... At the close of each of these four years, although my income has been comparatively great, I have had only a few shillings left. My needs are met each day by the help of God."

This does not mean that the Muellers lived in luxury. They felt strongly that the Lord meant it when He said, "Sell that ye

George Mueller...

have, and give alms" (Luke 12:33). Any extra things they had, they sold so that they could contribute more to the Lord's work.

George could hardly help noticing the many homeless boys and girls of his time. If they got into trouble, they were hauled off to jail and made to live with criminals. What could be done? Should he and Mary open a home for orphans? George prayed about it. He discussed the idea with friends. Even more important than wanting to care for orphans, he wanted to show that God could provide for such a place. He had seen people working far too hard to supply their needs rather than trusting the Lord. He wrote in his diary, "Everyone will see that God is faithful and answers prayer."[30]

At last, on December 5, 1835, he wrote, "This Scripture came alive to me today: 'Open thy mouth wide, and I will fill it' (Psalm 81:10). I was led to apply it to the orphan house and asked the Lord for a building, one thousand pounds, and suitable individuals to take care of the children." Two days later, on December 7, he wrote, "Today I received the first shilling for the orphan house."

Later he wrote, "During the next several weeks, God answered our prayers concerning the orphan house. We were given furniture, fabric, kitchen utensils, blankets, plates, and cups. . . . Several other people offered their services to work among the orphans, completely trusting God for their support."[31]

The day came in 1836 when George opened his home to the public. To his chagrin, no orphans showed up. It seemed strange of

---

30 Mueller, p. 73.
31 Mueller, p. 75.

... Quiet Faith in a Dependable God

the Lord. He had supplied everything—everything, that is, except children. Finally it hit George that this was one thing they had not asked for—children! Once they started praying for children, people brought them, just as they had brought everything else.

On the last day of 1837, George recorded that he was running three orphan houses, and nine workers were caring for eighty-one children. Ninety people, in other words, were counting on the Lord to supply each meal, simply in answer to prayer. George wrote, "Lord, Your servant is a poor man, but I have trusted in You and made my boast in You before the sons of men. Do not let me fail in this work!"[32]

People would ask George, "What will happen if the food does not come for a meal?" He would reply, "That can only happen if we fail to trust the Lord or if there is sin in our lives." Sometimes supplies would run extremely low. George would write in his diary entries like the following.

- ❖ February 5, 1842: "Now, at twelve o'clock, no means exist, as yet, to meet the expenses of the day."
- ❖ February 8: "Enough food is in all the houses for the meals of today. But we have not been able to buy any bread, and there is not enough money to buy milk tomorrow morning."
- ❖ February 19: "Saturday. Our money was again completely spent. Our provision stores were even more exhausted than on any previous Saturday."

---

32 Mueller, p. 89.

❖ March 17: "This morning our poverty, which now has lasted for several months, became exceeding great."

But he wrote triumphantly on May 10: "Our trials of faith during these seventeen months lasted longer and were sharper than during any previous period. Yet, the orphans had everything they needed in the way of nourishing food and clothing." How had God supplied it all? Often in little ways. Someone on his way to work had dropped in with a little money, or a worker had found unexpected cash in the offering box, or someone met George on a walk and gave him a gift, or a letter came with a donation.

One morning when the children came together to eat, the home had no food for them. But George led them in thanking God for the food anyway. Shortly there was a knock at the door. A local baker came in with loaves of bread, explaining that he had not been able to sleep the night before, so he got up early to make a donation to the home. Then came another knock! A milkman explained that his cart had broken down just outside their door and he had to unload his milk. So the children were well supplied. They always were; no child ever had to miss a meal for lack of food.

Should George open a fourth building? Someone had given a very large donation, as if the Lord were leading him in that direction. Besides, a neighbor was moving out of a house on the same street, making it available. George prayed about it for three weeks. Then he went to see if the house he had in mind was still available—and it wasn't! But the owners asked him to come back in another week. George merely prayed, "Lord, if *You* have no need of another Orphan House, *I* have none." A week later,

... Quiet Faith in a Dependable God

he checked again, and discovered that the owners had found another house to move into. The house was his.

The work kept on expanding. With donated money—George never borrowed—the orphanage bought a spacious property outside the city and built the first building. In 1849, the children moved to the new site.

Did George think that by this time he could sit back and watch God's provisions roll in? Not at all. God was leading him to put up another building. On November 12, 1857 he wrote, "I opened the house for four hundred more orphans today. How precious this was to me after praying every day for seven years."[33] By 1875, five buildings stood there, and the orphanage was caring for two thousand children.

George Mueller was no head-in-the-clouds dreamer. He calculated very carefully. But he believed that God was worthy of being included in his arithmetic. Early in his Christian life, he had trusted God with small amounts. As God proved Himself worthy of trust, he trusted God with more and more.

There is so much to be said about George Mueller. In later life, he traveled to forty-two countries and preached, sometimes several times a day. He told his audiences, "Do not think that I have the gift of faith. I only have the same kind of faith you can have, a faith that grew as I trusted the Lord."

---

33 Mueller, p. 227.

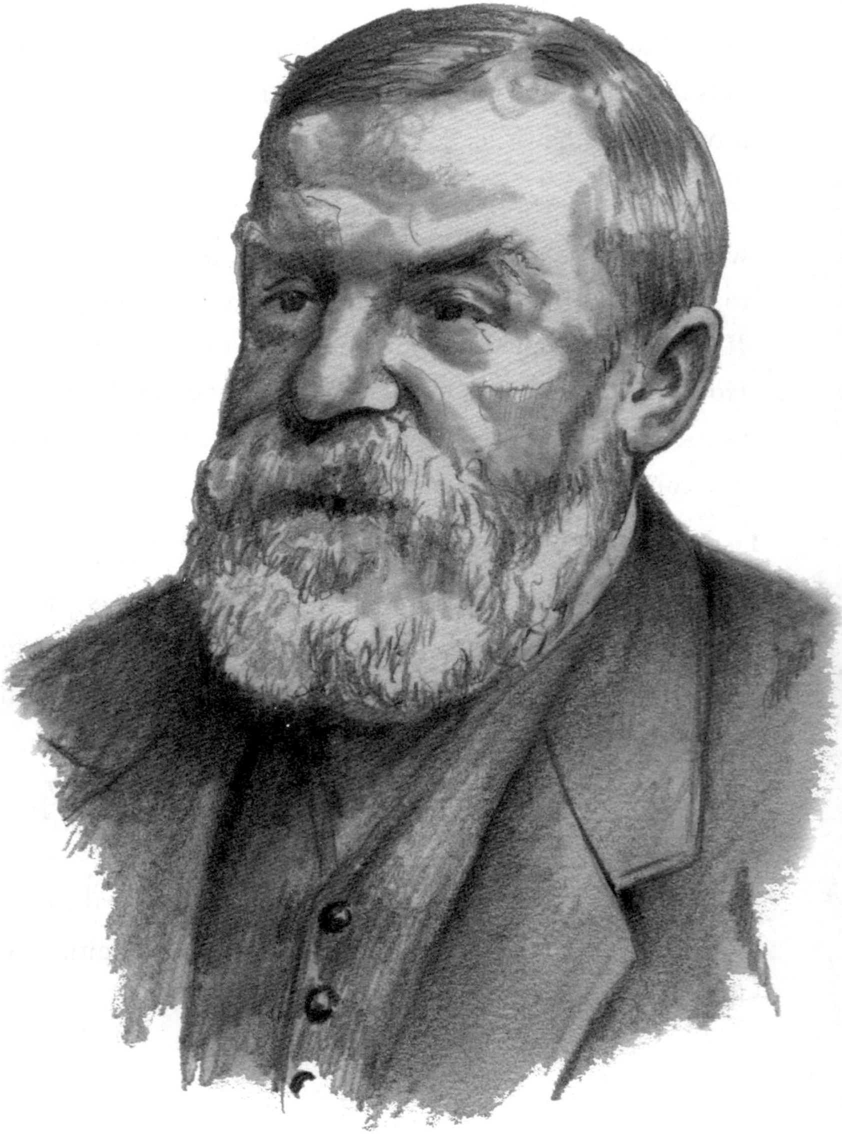

Dwight Moody

A Simple Gospel for Multitudes

(AD 1837–1899)

His name was Dwight Lyman Moody, but in those days men often went by their first two initials, so he called himself "D. L. Moody."

Dwight grew up in Northfield, Massachusetts. His father died when he was four, and his mother had her hands full raising the family. There was little time or money for extras. To save shoe leather, the boys would walk to church in bare feet, putting on their shoes when they came within sight of the church. Dwight's schooling ended when he was thirteen.

It was a strict home. Moody remembered, "When I was a boy, the Sabbath lasted from sundown on Saturday to sundown on Sunday, and I remember how we boys used to shout when it was over." On the other hand, in later years, he often told his

Dwight Moody ...

mother, "I thank you for making me go to the house of God when I didn't want to go."

At seventeen, Dwight went to Boston and became a clerk in his uncle's shoe store. One day, his Sunday school teacher dropped in at the store and found Dwight in the back, wrapping shoes. The teacher put his hand on Dwight's shoulder and a little awkwardly spoke of the Lord's love for him and the love he should give to the Lord. With this bit of encouragement, Dwight gave his heart to the Lord completely.

Not long after, Dwight moved to Chicago and became a successful shoe salesman there. But he wanted to do more than that. He rented a pew in his church and invited young men from the streets to worship there. After he had the pew filled, he rented another and another until he had filled five pews.

Later he found a struggling little Sunday school with sixteen teachers and twelve students. When he applied to teach there, he was told he would have to find his own students. Well, why not? This challenge was down Dwight's line. The next Sunday his class had eighteen children he had invited in from the streets. Not content, he invited still more until the building was crowded. Later he moved to another part of Chicago and did the same thing with a larger hall, and then a larger. The children loved him.

At first, public speaking did not go well for him. In fact, one deacon thought he should be satisfied to invite people in and let other workers do the speaking. "I know I make mistakes,"

Moody replied, "and I lack many things, but I'm doing the best I can with what I've got."

However, Moody had much to learn. He remembered, "I thought numbers were everything, and so I worked for numbers. When the attendance ran below one thousand, it troubled me; and when it ran to twelve or fifteen hundred, I was elated. Still none were converted; there was no harvest. Then God opened my eyes."

One Sunday when a regular teacher was ill, Moody filled in for him. He had a class of frivolous young ladies. "They laughed in my face," Moody remembered, "and I felt like opening the door and telling them all to get out and never come back." But that week, the regular teacher came and told Moody he did not expect to live long. Then, deeply troubled, he said, "I have never led any of my class to Christ. I really believe I have done the girls more harm than good." So the teacher and Moody went around to the homes of the various girls. One by one, they were able to lead them to faith in the Lord. The dying teacher finally had the assurance that he would meet his class again in glory.

Now Moody plunged into the greatest struggle of his life. Should he leave the business he loved and go into full-time Christian service for the sake of people he had learned to love even more than his business? After some days, he decided that he would take that step. "I have never regretted my choice," he said later. "Oh, the luxury of leading someone out of the

Dwight Moody . . .

darkness of this world into the glorious light and liberty of the Gospel!"

Moody's Sunday school was so successful that word about it spread. People traveled thousands of miles to find out how it was done. They invited him to come and help them set up Sunday schools.

Although Moody was never ordained, he began to preach. He did it so effectively that crowds came to hear him. He went on preaching tours, including tours to the British Isles. Often he took with him Gospel singer Ira Sankey. Perhaps Sankey's most notable moment came when he ran across Elizabeth Clephane's poem beginning, "There were ninety and nine that safely lay / In the shelter of the fold" and stuck it in his pocket. The poem had no music, but during the service that evening, Sankey suddenly realized that the poem in his pocket fit the service quite well. So when it was time for the music, he stepped to the organ, breathed a prayer, and began to sing, composing the tune of "The Ninety and Nine" as he went along. When he came to the end of the first verse, he was not quite sure he could sing the second verse the same way, but he did. People have been singing that song ever since.

One day in Dublin, Ireland, while Moody was sitting in a park with the evangelist Henry Varley, Mr. Varley said to him, "The world has yet to see what God can do with and for and through and in and by a man who is fully consecrated to Him." Moody said to himself, "I will try my utmost to be that man."

... A Simple Gospel for Multitudes

Moody preached very simply. He told stories that everyone could understand. He was warm and sincere. He believed the Bible and preached about God's love. People liked him, and crowds kept coming. Thousands of people gave their hearts to the Lord.

Moody's energy could get him into trouble. Once as he was welcoming a crowd to a service, a man stepped up to him and said something very insulting. Moody, being a burly fellow, gave the man a hard shove. To make matters worse, there was a short stairway just behind the man, and he tumbled down the stairs. The man was not badly hurt, but quite a number of people saw what happened. Some of them thought, "Moody is done. There is no way he can get up and talk about godly living this evening." When it was Moody's time to speak, he got up and in a trembling voice said, "Friends, before beginning tonight I want to confess that I yielded just now to my temper, out in the hall, and have done wrong. Just as I was coming in here tonight, I lost my temper with a man, and I want to confess my wrong before you all, and if that man is present here whom I thrust away from me in anger, I want to ask his forgiveness and God's. Let us pray." He spoke as usual, and if anything, God touched people's hearts more than usual.

Moody sometimes preached to audiences of tens of thousands of people. Once at the Crystal Palace in Glasgow, Scotland, the place was so packed that twenty or thirty thousand people, including Moody himself, could not find a way in. So

Dwight Moody . . .

he preached from the seat of a cab, and the choir led the singing from the roof of a nearby shed.[34]

However, Moody was not a man to crow about his huge audiences. When he was asked about numbers of people who attended or confessed Christ, he had very little to say. He wished newspapers would report less about what Moody did and more about what Lord did. Other preachers besides himself preached at his campaigns, and Moody was delighted to take notes on their good points and illustrations.

Once he remarked about a meeting in Brooklyn, "There was a hush in that meeting, and a power, that we have seldom had for twenty or thirty years, from the time it began until we got through. It was a hot day in July, when people think nothing can be done, but that audience was just as if it was held by some unseen power, and it seemed as if God Almighty was speaking to the people."

---

[34] In reflecting on Moody's revivals, *The Nation* magazine stated,

"We are told of the huge crowds, sometimes 20,000 people, who come to the Moody and Sankey revival meetings, and of the enormous sales of the *Gospel Hymns*. The number of copies printed is reported to be 50,000,000.

"Such revival services we are not likely to see again . . . and this method of appeal is now gravely distrusted even in denominations which once relied on it. Mr. Moody himself in his later years is said to have doubted whether the effect of the revivals was permanent. He found that, after the excitement had died out, the tears and groans from 'conviction of sin' and the ecstasies of conversion left many men about where they were before, only a little more indifferent and callous. A community 'burnt over' by a wild revival often proved a difficult field to cultivate by sober and steady means." *The Nation*, August 20, 1908, as quoted by Joseph and Christian Stoll, *The Songs We Sing* (Aylmer, ON: Pathway Publishers, 1995) pp. 21–22.

. . . A Simple Gospel for Multitudes

D. L. Moody was not only a great evangelist but also a talented organizer. He founded Moody Bible Institute in Chicago, where people still prepare for various fields of Christian service.

At last, while holding a campaign in Kansas City, he was stricken with serious heart trouble. Taken home to die at age sixty-two, he said, "This is my triumph; this is my coronation day! I have been looking forward to it for years."

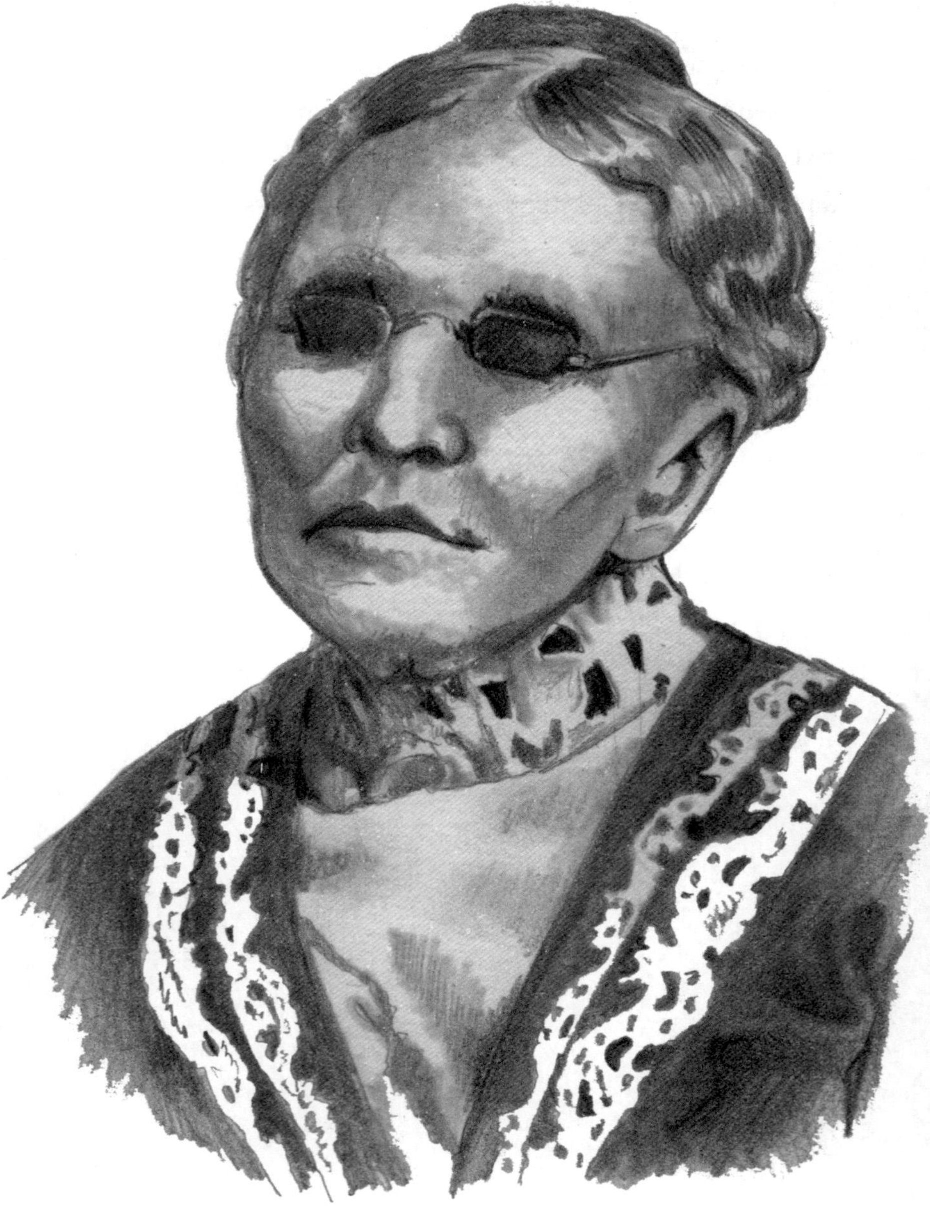

Fanny Crosby

A Poet Who Gave Herself Away

(AD 1820–1915)

Nearly everyone who knows about Fanny Crosby knows she was blind, but not everyone knows that she was born with perfectly good eyes. When she was six weeks old, however, her eyes became inflamed, and a well-meaning doctor prescribed a hot compress. The compress must have been hot indeed, for after that Fanny never could see again. When Fanny was five, her mother took her to see a doctor, hoping he could restore her vision, but after he examined her eyes, he said they were permanently damaged.

"Poor little girl," the doctor said, patting her head, but Fanny did not like his pity. She had learned that life has many satisfactions, even for the blind. Her first poem, when she was eight years old, ran, "Oh, what a happy child I am / Although I cannot see! / I am resolved that in this world / Contented I will

Fanny Crosby...

be / How many blessings I enjoy / That other people don't; / To weep or sigh because I'm blind / I cannot and I won't."

Besides, she did not altogether live in darkness. Her eyes were like frosted windows, through which she could see some light. Once in later years, a friend was describing a sunset to her. She assured him she understood, and added, "I can see it too!"

But for any other kind of seeing, she had to use the eyes of her mind. When someone described the twinkling stars or milkweed floating through space, she used her vivid imagination. She also learned to notice through hearing, feeling, smelling, and tasting—things that people with ordinary sight miss.

Her mother and grandmother both read to her. When Fanny was nine, the family moved from New York state to Connecticut. There they made a new friend, a Mrs. Hawley, who taught Fanny much of the Bible. Fanny wrote later, "Because of her help, by the time I reached the age of ten, I could recite the first five books of the Old Testament, many Psalms, and much of the New Testament."

Still, struggles came her way. As a girl, Fanny was troubled because so many good things in life seemed to be just beyond her reach. She had a curious mind, but how could she fill it? How could she be useful in life if she could not even read and write? Fanny often prayed about this and was thrilled when the way opened for her to go to a school for the blind in New York City.

When she arrived at the school, after her first homesickness, she excelled in most subjects. There were exceptions—she found

...A Poet Who Gave Herself Away

reading by Braille to be slow and difficult, and her mind balked at arithmetic. For a while the school excused her from arithmetic, but a new supervisor insisted that she learn. He also called her aside and kindly explained to her that her skill in composing poems could become a snare to her if she let people's comments make her feel too good about herself.

Wiping her tears, Fanny thanked him, and she tried hard to focus on her studies. In fact, for six years she composed no poetry. She was rewarded for her self-discipline when arithmetic finally made sense to her. Still, she felt the nudge to create poetry, which she kept trying to squelch.

One day a phrenologist visited school. He believed that by feeling student's heads, he could tell them what talents they had. When Fanny's turn came, he exclaimed, "Here is a poet!" He encouraged the supervisor to help her all he could. Since phrenology is really not accurate enough to be called a science, we may guess that God used the phrenologist to serve His own purposes. After that, the supervisor encouraged Fanny to use her poetical talent. Even though she took up poetry again, Fanny did well enough in her studies that she finally became a teacher.

In the spring of 1849, cholera struck New York City. The school sent as many students home as possible, but Fanny chose to stay. She worked in a nearby hospital.

Some of her students died, and Fannie was overcome with doubts and fears. What if she had died? What, after all, was her relationship with the Lord? The church she had grown up with did not seem to answer her questions, so she began attending a church where people worshiped in a warmer, livelier style. Several times when an invitation was given, she went forward, but she could not seem to find peace with God.

The last time, she went forward alone. There she knelt before the Lord until the congregation began singing an old hymn by Isaac Watts: "Alas, and Did My Saviour Bleed." When they got to the words, "Here, Lord, I give myself away; / 'Tis all that I can do," Fanny had her answer. At that moment, she gave herself completely to the Lord. Afterward, she remarked that she "had been trying to hold the world in one hand and the Lord in the other."

When she was thirty-seven, Fanny married a blind friend whose name was Alexander van Alstyne. They had one baby, who died, and no other children. But people do not remember Fanny for her marriage so much as for her poetry.

The latter 1800s were the days of great revival meetings, evangelists, singers, and Gospel hymns. Fanny became acquainted with various Gospel poets and composers and worked along with them. She wrote thousands of poems until she could not remember them all. No one knows how many she wrote, since she wrote under various pen names for various publishers.

Sometimes poetry would come to her quite rapidly. A friend named Phoebe Knapp played for Fanny a tune she had composed, and Fanny exclaimed, "That says, 'Blessed Assurance, Jesus Is Mine!'" When another friend, William Howard Doane, hummed a tune for her, she clapped her hands and said, "Why, that says, 'Safe in the Arms of Jesus.' After a short prayer, for

... A Poet Who Gave Herself Away

she always prayed before she composed poetry, she dictated the words while he wrote the hymn.

Publishers gave Fanny very little pay for her poetry, but Fanny did not complain. She would have been poor anyway, for when she had any extra money, she gave it away. There were so many needs! For some years, Fanny and her husband lived just down the street from some of the worst slums in New York. She loved the people there and tried to lead them to the Lord. She took part in services held there. At least once, she went forward along with someone responding to an invitation. Out of her experiences came songs like "Rescue the Perishing" and "Pass Me Not, O Gentle Saviour."

When Fanny was seventy-four, she wrote one of her last well-known poems, "Saved by Grace." It begins, "Some day the silver cord will break, / And I no more as now shall sing; / But, oh, the joy when I shall wake / Within the palace of the King!" Composer George Stebbins gave it a slow, sweet, thoughtful melody, and people have loved it ever since.

Fanny was an elderly lady by this time, but she lived another twenty years, composing poetry and helping people where she could. If people on the street saw a stooped old lady in old clothes and tattered bonnet, they knew it was probably Fanny. When she died at age ninety-four, her work ceased, but her songs live on.

> "God gives everyone memory, but most people with sight lose it through laziness."
>
> —*Fanny Crosby*

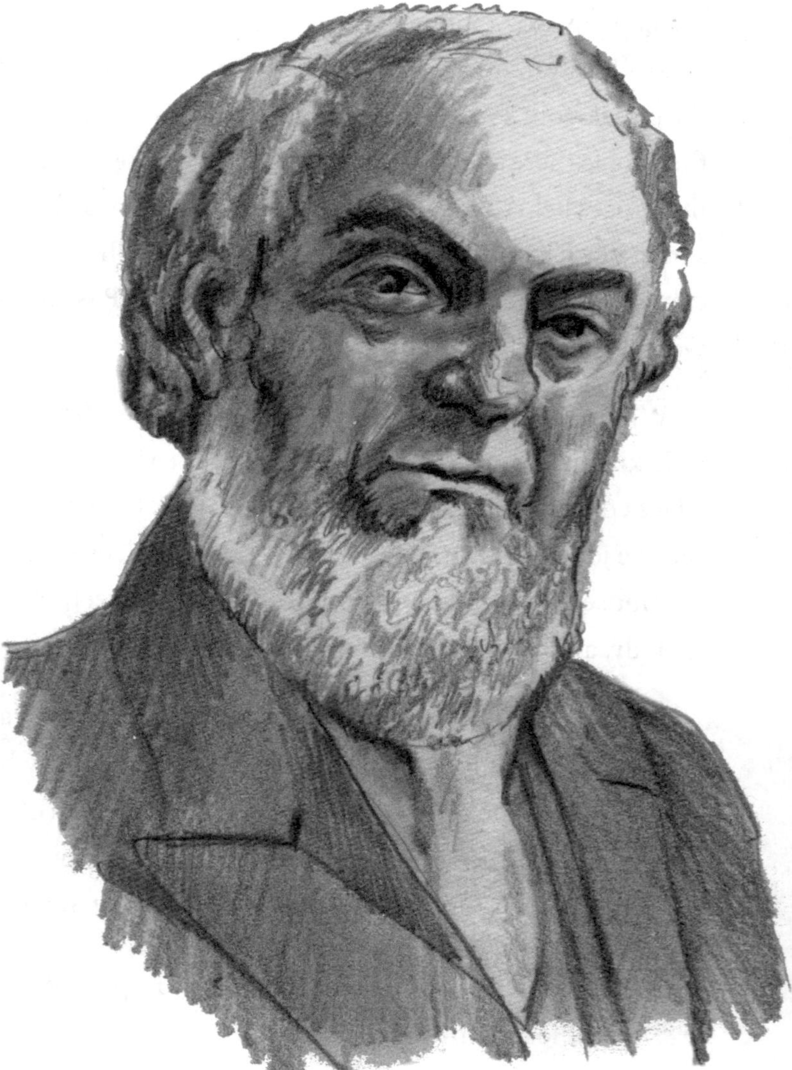

Charles Taze Russell

Founder of Jehovah's Witnesses

(AD 1852–1916)

Haberdashery is a big word, but it simply means a men's clothing store. Charles Russell's father was a haberdasher in the area of Pittsburgh, Pennsylvania, and Charles grew up familiar with the business. He went to school for only seven years, which was not unusual in the mid-1800s, and quit about age fourteen.

As a youth, he had a terrible fear of hell and would go around writing on sidewalks to warn people about it. But at age seventeen, he had a long talk with someone who convinced him there was no literal hell.

When he was eighteen, he wandered into a church where the people were discussing the Second Coming of Christ, and he became fascinated with the subject. In his spare time, Charles

Charles Taze Russell ...

would study the Bible along with Hebrew and Greek dictionaries, hoping to gain a better grasp on the Bible's hidden meanings. Around age twenty, he began teaching his own Bible classes.

Charles must have had a convincing way of teaching. In 1874, when he was still in his early twenties, his group elected him pastor, although he was never ordained.

As his theology developed, he came out quite differently from the Christians around him. Here are some of his points.

- All the churches are rejected by God.
- All governments are under Satan and should be resisted.
- There is no literal hell. Wicked people will be annihilated somewhat like a soap bubble; they will not suffer forever.
- There is no Trinity—that is a doctrine fit for the Dark Ages.
- Jesus Christ was created and is not God.
- Christ did not physically rise from the dead. Charles wrote, "Our Lord's human body ... did not decay or corrupt ... Whether it was dissolved into gases or whether it is still preserved somewhere ... no one knows."[35]
- Christ will not return physically, and there will be no physical resurrection of the dead.
- Christ returned spiritually in 1874 (the year Charles was elected pastor), bringing in the millennium, which is the thousand years of peace predicted in Revelation 20.

---

35 *Studies in the Scriptures*, Vol. II, p. 129, cited in Walter Martin, *The Kingdom of the Cults* (Minneapolis, MN: Bethany House Publishers, 1985), p. 59.

... Founder of Jehovah's Witnesses

In his late twenties, Charles started up a periodical known as the *Watch Tower*. This periodical is still published today by the millions in many languages, along with another periodical called *Awake!*

Charles's preaching drew crowds. His movement spread rapidly, and in 1908 Charles moved headquarters to New York City. But he was having some personal problems.

In 1879 he had married a woman named Maria Ackley and appointed her secretary-treasurer of the society. She helped him edit the *Watch Tower*. However, in 1903, she sued for divorce because of "his conceit, egotism, domination, and improper conduct to other women."

In late 1911, Charles Russell undertook a tour of the world. He published the sermons that he claimed to have preached at various places, and he put out reports saying he had been enthusiastically received. But people who knew the facts said that in many of these places he had never preached.

Charles Russell seems to have been eager to make money however he could. He began advertising "miracle wheat," which was supposed to produce five times as much as ordinary wheat. He charged a dollar a pound, which was no small price in those days. But a newspaper, the *Brooklyn Daily Eagle,* published a cartoon making fun of Russell and his wheat. Stung, Russell sued the newspaper for $100,000. The paper retorted, "The *Eagle* goes even further and declares that at the trial it will show that 'Pastor' Russell's religious cult is nothing more than a money-making scheme." In January 1913, government experts who had tested the "miracle wheat" testified in court that there was nothing outstanding about it. Russell lost his suit.

Charles Taze Russell ...

In 1912, a Baptist pastor named J. J. Ross wrote a pamphlet sharply accusing Russell of being "neither a scholar nor a theologian," and giving reasons why. Russell sued Ross, and on March 17, 1913, the court looked at Ross's accusations one by one. At one point, an attorney asked Russell if he could read the Greek alphabet.

"Oh, yes," said Russell.

The attorney asked, "Can you tell me the correct letters if you see them?"

Russell replied, "Some of them, I might make a mistake on some of them."

The attorney asked, "Would you tell me the names of those on top of the page, page 447 I have got here?"

Russell said, "Well, I don't know that I would be able to."

So it went during the five hours of questioning. Russell had claimed to be ordained, but now he admitted that he never was. He swore that his wife had not divorced him, but then was forced by evidence to admit that she had. Needless to say, Russell lost the suit.

More trouble followed. Charles taught that forty years after Christ's invisible coming in 1874, God's kingdom would come in power. He wrote, "The final end of the kingdoms of this world, and the full establishment of the kingdom of God, will be accomplished by the end of AD 1914." His followers waited eagerly for this to happen. Indeed, in 1914 many nations rushed into World War I, so it was true that great events took place that year, but not the wonderful things Charles Russell had predicted. Many of his followers were shaken and left his faith.

Still, Russell kept moving and spreading his doctrines. Active to the last, he died on a train while traveling in Texas. J. F. Rutherford, a right-hand man of his who had served as Russel's lawyer, took the helm. Rutherford later became noted for his famous declaration, "Millions now living will never die."

Rutherford helped Russell's followers by changing their name. They had been called Russellites, but that name struck people wrong if they knew something about Charles Russell. So their new name, beginning in 1931, was Jehovah's Witnesses.

Today Jehovah's Witnesses, JWs for short, continue to worship in churches they call Kingdom Halls. Their church windows are few and small, but that is just for practicality—windows are expensive to put in and hard to defend from vandals and burglars, so why not invest in something more worthwhile? They use their own version of the Bible, commonly called the *New World Translation*. They believe most of the same doctrines that Charles Russell taught—no hell, no physical return of the Lord, and so on. They go out two by two to share their faith, and they give out free literature (*Awake!* on top and *Watch Tower* underneath). Most of them are pleasant and eager to talk about Scripture, whether they knock on your door or you knock on theirs. However, unlike the Mormons, who mistakenly revere Joseph Smith, the Jehovah's Witnesses would be quite happy to forget about Charles Taze Russell.

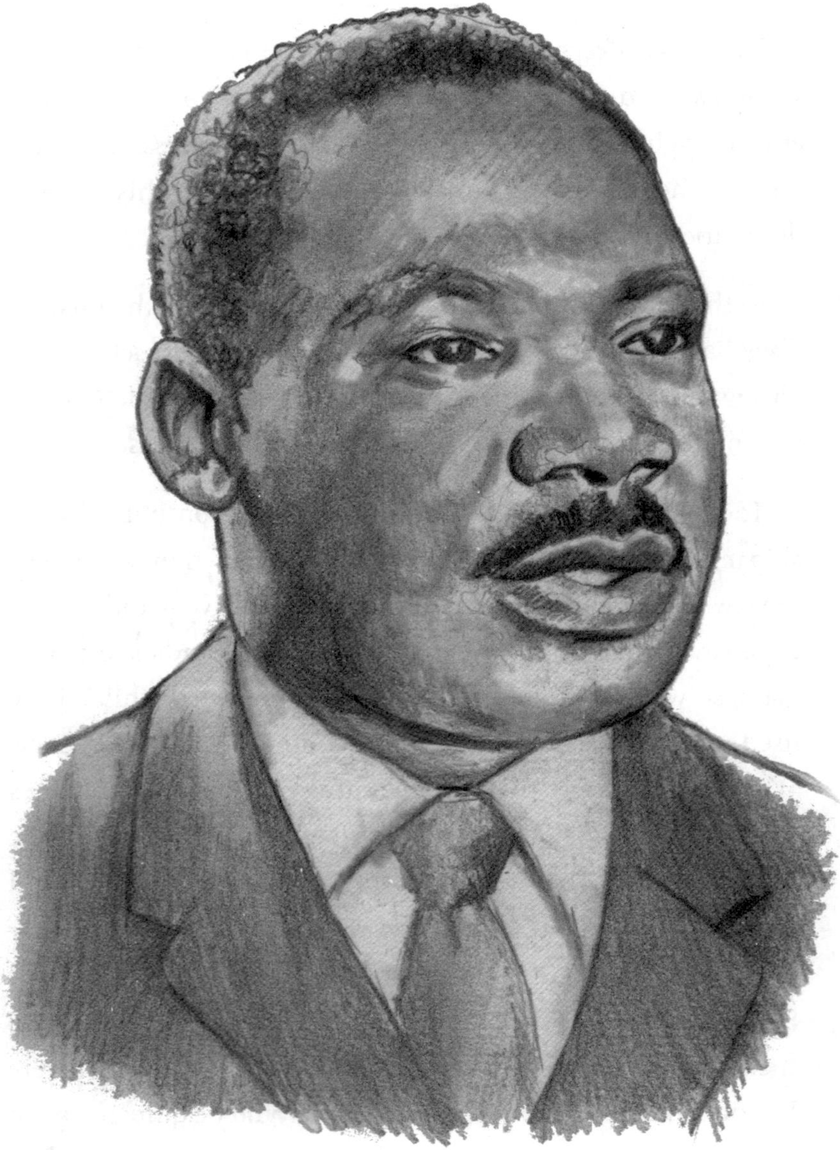

Martin Luther King, Jr.

Civil Rights Leader

(AD 1929–1968)

After the Civil War, many black people were no better off than before.[36] For one thing, all but two of the major battles had taken place in the South. The Northern armies had devastated the South, killing men and livestock and destroying transportation and communication systems. As the South struggled to survive after the war, many larger landowners broke their farmland into small sections. These they leased to

---

36 In August of 1863, President Lincoln had met with black leaders, offering to help them colonize a place of their own in Central America. He told them the United States government would support and protect any colonies, but for the most part, black leaders declined. The two colonies which were started, one in Haiti and the other in Panama, were unable to remain self-sufficient. (Williams [2006] "Doing Less" and "Doing More," pp. 54–59;

Allen Guelzo, *Abraham Lincoln, Redeemer President,* (Grand Rapids, MI: W. B. Eerdmans, 1999), pp 333–335;

Bruce Catton, *Terrible Swift Sword,* (Garden City, NY: Doubleday, 1963), pp. 365–367, 461–468)

former slaves or to poorer white people, who would receive a share of the crop. However, as cotton prices plunged, both the sharecroppers and landowners faced poverty and ruin.

Adding to the tensions, a rumor circulated that the Freedmen's Bureau[37] had promised every former slave forty acres of land and a mule. When they did not receive this, some blacks accused anyone more fortunate than themselves of having withheld from them their just dues.[38]

Through Reconstruction, the United States government tried to slowly re-integrate the Southern states while helping African Americans find their place among whites in society. Numerous other forms of aid were extended to them.[39]

However, the slaves, suddenly free, often lacked the needed resources and education—and sometimes the motivation. Some had learned that pressure tactics and a dramatic recounting of one's wrongs were easier ways to get ahead than working or climbing upward by merit.

The struggle with the new order extended even to worship.[40]

---

37 An arm of the Northern occupation army in the South
38 Although this rumor proved to be false, the agency did spend five million dollars to educate blacks, in addition to other help.
39 After the war, northern missionaries founded numerous private academies and colleges across the South for freedmen. In addition, every state founded state colleges for freedmen, such as Alcorn State University in Mississippi.
40 "In a highly controversial move, the Northern Methodists had used the Army to seize control of Methodist churches in large cities, over the vehement protests of the Southern Methodists" (Ralph E. Morrow, "Northern Methodism in the South During Reconstruction," *Mississippi Valley Historical Review* [1954] pp. 197–218.
　　Daniel Stowell, *Rebuilding Zion: The Religious Reconstruction of the South, 1863–1877*, (New York, NY: Oxford University Press, 1998), pp. 30–31

The Freedmen's Bureau worked out a quota system to put African Americans into public office. Fifteen hundred blacks held office under this arrangement. Over one hundred black ministers were elected to state legislatures during Reconstruction, as well as several to Congress and one, Hiram Revels, to the U.S. Senate.

Some non-Christian Southerners, bitter at the devastation wreaked upon their land, pushed back with campaigns of segregation and terror.

In the South, Jim Crow laws, as they were called, were enacted which kept black and white people "separate but equal." Eventually, everything was separate—restrooms, drinking fountains, telephone booths, even the Bibles on which they swore in court. Unfortunately, facilities were seldom equal.

It was hard for a black person to find a job as well paying as a white person could get. Talented people could not easily get ahead.

In southern courts, a white man's word was often taken over a black man's.

Into this situation came Martin Luther King Jr.

He was the son of a minister in Atlanta, Georgia. A bright student who skipped grades nine and twelve, King went on to college, where he met Coretta Scott. She became his wife in 1953. He began serving as a pastor in Montgomery, Alabama, despite his refusal to believe in the deity of Christ, as well as various other tenets of faith held dear by Christians.[41] In becoming a pastor, he followed the path of many of his forbears who wished to gain political recognition.[42]

He said of his school days, "I went to high school on the other side of town—to the Booker T. Washington High School. I had to get the bus in what was known as the Fourth Ward and ride over to the West Side. In those days, rigid patterns of segregation existed on the buses, so that Negroes had to sit in the backs of buses. Whites were seated in the front, and often if whites didn't get on the buses, those seats were still reserved for whites only, so Negroes had to stand over empty seats. I would end up having to go to the back of that bus with my body, but every time I got on that bus I left my mind up on the front seat. And I said to myself, 'One of these days, I'm going to put my body up there where my mind is.' "[43]

In 1955, a Montgomery woman named Rosa Parks, a seamstress and secretary of the Montgomery NAACP,[44] boarded a bus on the way home from work and sat in the section reserved for black people. Later a white man boarded the bus, which was full, and the driver asked several black passengers on a

---

[41] King was skeptical of many of Christianity's claims. At the age of thirteen, he denied the bodily resurrection of Jesus during Sunday school. From this point, he stated, "doubts began to spring forth unrelentingly." However, he said later that the Bible has many profound truths which one cannot escape, and decided to enter seminary (*An Autobiography of Religious Development*—The Martin Luther King Jr. Research and Education Institute).

[42] As stated by Charles H. Pearce (1817 to 1887), an AME minister in Florida: "A man in this State cannot do his whole duty as a minister except he looks out for the political interests of his people" (Foner, *Reconstruction* (1988), p. 93).

[43] Clayborne Carson, *The Autobiography of Martin Luther King, Jr.*, ed., (New York, NY: Warner Books, Inc., 1998), p. 9., Morgan, p. 555.

[44] National Association for the Advancement of Colored People

... Civil Rights Leader

seat just behind the white section to stand in order to give the new passenger a seat. Rosa's seatmates got up, but she refused. The driver called the police; two of them boarded the bus and arrested Rosa Parks, who was told she had to pay a fine.

In response, Martin Luther King Jr. helped to organize a bus boycott. Black people of Montgomery found other ways to get to work. They carpooled. They raised money to buy station wagons. Hundreds walked. The bus company could not afford to run buses. Some places were bombed during the boycott, including King's house. The struggle worked its way up through the courts until the Supreme Court decided that segregation on the Montgomery buses was illegal.

King tried hard to remain nonviolent, although he believed that black Americans, as well as other disadvantaged Americans, should receive money because their ancestors had been wronged. His thinking was influenced by Mohandas Gandhi, who had used nonviolent methods to win freedom for India from the British. His nonviolence was a political approach rather than a matter of conscience. King was frequently protected by other civil rights activists who carried guns.

In 1963, blacks in the steel-producing city of Birmingham, Alabama, protested segregation. Even school children became involved. King himself wrote the famous "Letter From a Birmingham Jail." In it, he explained his goals and defended what he was doing.

Later that year, King went to Washington, D.C., to support a demonstration there. As he spoke to the people who had gathered at the Washington Monument, he made his famous "I have a dream" speech. "I have a dream," he said, "that my four little children will one day live in a nation where they will not be judged by the color of their skin but by the content of their character.... That one day ... little black boys and black girls will be able to join hands with little white boys and white girls as brothers and sisters."

In this speech, also expanding on the theme that others owed them something, King described the promises made by America as a "promissory note" on which America had defaulted. He said that "America has given the Negro people a bad check," but that "we've come to cash this check" by marching in Washington, D.C.[45]

King was a busy man, and we have mentioned briefly only a few typical events that took place in his short life. In 1968, King went to Memphis, Tennessee, to support a strike of black sanitation workers. In a speech on April 3, he said, "I don't know what will happen now. We've got some difficult days ahead. But it really doesn't matter now, because I've been to the mountaintop."

The next day, as King stood on a motel balcony talking to friends, a rifle shot from across the street took his life. He was thirty-nine years old. Despairing black people rioted in over a hundred American cities.

---

[45] See David A. Bobbit, *The Rhetoric of Redemption, Kenneth Burk's Redemption Drama and Martin Luther King Jr's "I Have a Dream Speech"* (Lanham, MD: Rowman & Littlefield, 2004).

Another black man named Tom Skinner, who said he admired King in many ways, said this: "But Martin Luther King had one philosophy that I disagreed with, and which I think is the entire downfall of liberalism in American society, and that is that he believed in the innate 'good' of all men; he believed that all men were good basically, and that it was just a matter of creating the circumstances and the situation to bring the good out of men. . . . He missed one important fact, and that is that man must be regenerated, his attitudes must be changed, a revolution must first occur within his heart, before it can occur in society." Tom meant that true goodness is found only in one who surrenders his entire being to God, not in one who quotes only certain Scriptures and selectively uses certain godly principles, such as nonviolence, to advance his causes.

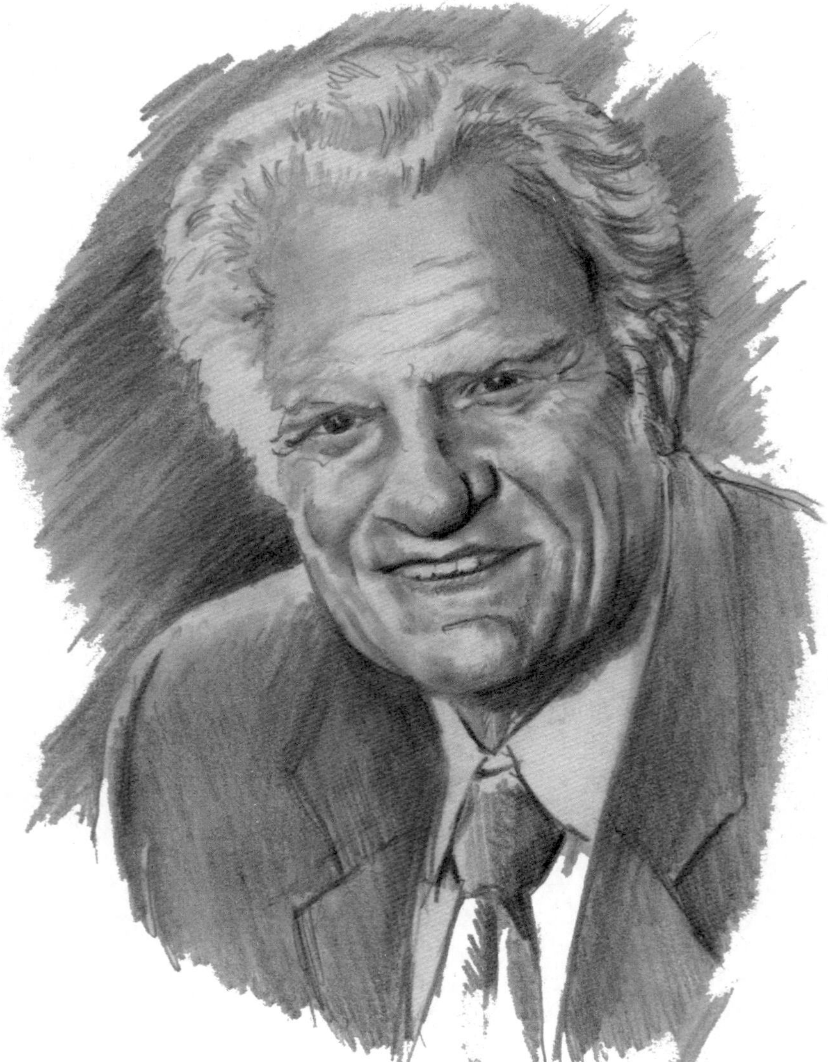

BILLY GRAHAM

INTERNATIONAL EVANGELIST

(AD 1918–2018)

"There is no such thing as truth." "Anything goes!" "What's wrong with drugs?" "Maybe suicide is the answer for some people." "God is dead."

How did people come up with ideas like these? They listened to philosophers who did away with clear Bible terms like *sin, hell, condemnation*, and *salvation through Jesus' blood*. Instead, they used nice-sounding but gray words like *reform, optimism, social betterment, friendship*, and *improvement*.

Naturally, not everyone agreed. Some church leaders rose up and defended the old, solid doctrines of the faith. Many of them became known as Fundamentalists because they stood for the basics that Christians had always believed in. This does not mean the Fundamentalists believed and taught everything just right. In fact, on many points they disagreed with each

Billy Graham...

other. But on certain basics they stood together and raised their voices to say so.

The most famous such voice was that of Billy Graham. Billy was born in North Carolina. His parents were members of the Associate Reformed Presbyterian Church and knew what they believed. As a youth, Billy gave his heart to the Lord, and later he rededicated his life to Him. In time, he became a preacher.

But Billy faced challenges to his faith. He had a friend named Charles Templeton who was also a preacher. Charles was as talented as Billy, but he had more and more doubts about God. Finally Charles left the church and wrote a book called *Farewell to God*.

Templeton's challenges shook Billy, who took time out to think about his friend's arguments. The night came in 1947 when Billy knew he had come to an important turning point in his life. In his own words, "I got my Bible and went out in the moonlight, and I came to a stump. I placed my Bible on the stump and knelt down and said, 'O God, I cannot answer some of the questions Chuck and some of the other people are raising, but I accept this book by faith as the Word of God.'"

Audiences gladly heard what Billy had to say. Here was a man who, like Moody, preached a very simple, direct, factual, emphatic message! He preached it straight from a book he believed in—the Bible. He would say, "The Bible says," and to many people it came like a breath of fresh air. Billy's message

... International Evangelist

would begin with sin, condemnation, and hell. Then he would point to the cross, repentance, and the way heavenward.

Billy Graham tried not to get involved in doctrinal disputes. He didn't spend time on social improvement. He just preached salvation by faith in Jesus Christ.

Billy preached to larger and larger crowds. He used modern forms of communication to help him. Since most people in the crowd were too far away to see him well, his face was projected onto a huge screen. In 1995, he preached to a greater audience than ever before with the help of thirty-seven satellites. For three nights he preached in San Juan, Puerto Rico. A team of translators put his message into 117 languages. The program reached millions of people around the world who had gathered in groups of thousands—in stadiums, churches, huge tents, or even open fields—wherever there was a satellite dish.

This was not just a one-man show. A host of people around the world took part in prayer meetings, served as counselors, and followed up after persons responded to the invitation to follow Christ.

Billy reached still more millions through the television networks that beamed his message directly into people's homes.[46] No doubt many people who made commitments fell away, but others stuck to them.

---

46 On October 15, 1989 Graham received a star on the Hollywood Walk of Fame. Graham was the only minister, functioning in that capacity, to receive one. Stolberg, Sheryl (October 16, 1989). "Billy Graham Now a Hollywood Star" *Los Angeles Times*.

Billy Graham ...

How do we explain why so many thousands of people responded to his ministry? One observer said, "Billy Graham is perhaps the most prayed-for man on earth today." Another said, "Billy is the most focused man on prayer I ever knew. Each time he called me as a crusade director, he began with, 'How's prayer?' Billy himself told a friend he took every chance he had to pray, whether he was driving, flying, or talking to someone.

However, Billy did things that left many godly people bewildered. How could he offer the opening prayers at the Democratic and the Republican National Conventions, as he did in 1968?[47]

How could he go to combat areas and tell the American soldiers, "I come to bring you greetings from millions of Americans who are proud of you and what you are doing"?[48,49]

Let's put it this way. God uses all kinds of people for His own purposes. A number of "great figures" we looked at in this book had serious faults, and Billy had his. There is no point in our imitating other people's mistakes; we make enough of our own. Rather let us say what good about them we can and seek to avoid their errors.

Perhaps Billy Graham summed it up the best, not only for himself but for many other people. "If we have accomplished

---

[47] Donald Kraybill, *Our Star-Spangled Faith* (Scottdale, PA: Herald Press, 1976), p. 70.
[48] Sherwood Eliot Wirt, *Billy* (Wheaton, IL: Crossway Books, 1997), p. 151.
[49] Graham has been outspoken against communism and supported the American Cold War policy, including the Vietnam War.

anything at all . . . it has only been because of the grace and mercy of God."

Finally, all that Billy Graham, or any other teacher, has taught must be weighed against Biblical teachings. "Prove all things; hold fast that which is good" (1 Thessalonians 5:21).

HENRY'S DOZING

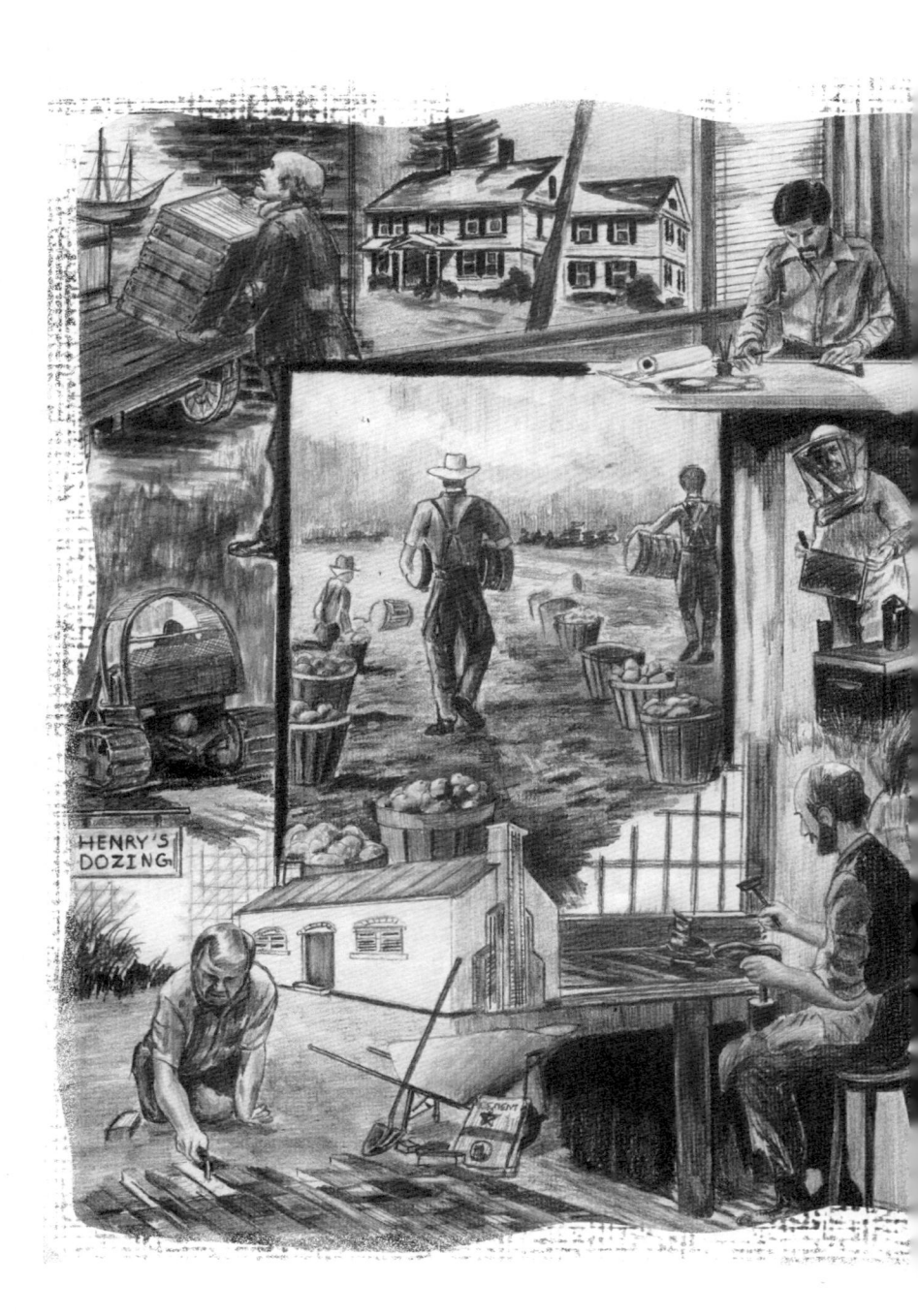

The Forgotten Figures of History

Who was the greatest janitor who ever lived?

At first that seems like a silly question, for whoever heard of a great janitor—or, for that matter, a great water pourer, shoe polisher, pigtail maker, or tract-hander-outer?

Well, that all depends on what we mean by "great."

The word *great* in the title of this book means "outstanding," "well known," "famous," "influential," "exceptional." These are perfectly good synonyms for *great*.

But there is another way of deciding who is great—God's way. Remember what Jesus did when His disciples asked Him, "Who is the greatest in the kingdom of heaven?" He set a child among them and said, "Whosoever therefore shall humble himself as

The Forgotten Figures of History

this little child, the same is greatest in the kingdom of heaven" (Matthew 18:4).

Now we have new words for *great*. Humble. Kind. Loving. Trusting. Honest. These are the people that God calls great.

Some people were both kinds of great. They were called great by both God and men. They were famous, but they were humble too. They were well known, but they would have given all their fame away just to be true Christians.

Other people were only one kind of great—the wrong kind. In this book we call them great, but only because they were famous and influential. They were far from great in God's sight.

Still other people—and there were millions of these—were great in God's sight only. We have not included them in the book because we have never heard of them. But God heard and saw, and to them that was all that mattered.

Many of these people worked behind the scenes as helpers. Famous authors needed un-famous editors and printers. Famous evangelists needed people who invited friends to the meetings. Famous Bible translators needed wives and sons and daughters who would help them, sometimes by knowing when to leave them alone.

Many people were helpers of helpers. They pulled weeds, cleaned windows, poured water, set up folding chairs, tied children's shoes, and answered questions. If nothing else, they sat where the usher told them to sit.

The Forgotten Figures of History

Some of the greatest people knew how to work behind the scenes themselves. They studied alone, they sat on committees, they talked to neighbors, they prayed. Certainly they had their moments of fame, but mostly they plugged away in the quietness while the clock ticked.

God bless them all. And, unknown readers, God bless you all.

Herein lies the most important thing: if we work hand in hand and heart in heart with Jesus Christ, it is all great, even if we are only helping to pass the salt around the table.

> I know a lasting record stands
> Inscribed against my name . . .
> For glory or for shame.